Bad Sex in Kentucky

A MEMOIR

Kevin Lane Dearinger

Bad Sex in Kentucky

RABBIT HOUSE PRESS
Versailles, KY 40383

First Paperback Edition by Rabbit House Press October 2019

Edited by: Erin Chandler
Cover & Interior Design: Brooke Lee
Cover Photo: Kevin Lane Dearinger
Author Photo: Kevin Lane Dearinger

Published in the United States by Rabbit House Press

Printed in the United States of America

ISBN-13: 978-0-578-58855-1

To Pam Dearinger Hutton and David Bernard Dearinger,
because we are bound soul to soul to soul.

With gratitude to F. Kathleen Foley Herder, Shirley Brown Pierce, Celia Tackaberry, Ken Billington, Anne Rogers and Mike Hall, Darrell Ung, Maria Blazer and Judith Blazer Kaufman, Andy Sandberg, Linda Lane Haynes, Gail Kennedy, Danny Mizell, Martin Moran, John Brian Quinn, David Elledge, Mary Baker and Donna Gardt, Shayne Brakefield, Bob Morgan, Jon Coleman, Tuesday G. Meadows, Maury Sparrow, Jim Gray, Lance Poston, Fr. Jon Buffington, Erin Chandler, Alan Gooch and his numerous predecessors, and all my former students.

With thanks, as well, to Third Street Stuff, Lexington, Kentucky, and Starbucks, here and there, for offering me strong tea and a place to write.

Above all, with love for my family, all of them, including Arnetta Winkfield Hill. And especially my parents, John Arthur and Anna Louise Lane Dearinger, who, with love, taught me what they knew of love. I miss them both in every distant train whistle and every rising moon.

Mother read an early draft of the opening chapters of this work and objected only to the use of metaphor. Things, she argued, are only like themselves, and comparisons are, at best, misleading.

William Shakespeare's Kentucky Sonnet

CXXIX

The expense of spirit in a waste of shame
Is lust in action: and till action, lust
Is perjured, murderous, bloody, full of blame,
Savage, extreme, rude, cruel, not to trust;
Enjoyed no sooner but despised straight;
Past reason hunted; and no sooner had,
Past reason hated, as a swallowed bait,
On purpose laid to make the taker mad.
Mad in pursuit and in possession so;
Had, having, and in quest to have extreme;
A bliss in proof, and proved, a very woe;
Before, a joy proposed; behind a dream.
All this the world well knows; yet none knows well
To shun the heaven that leads men to this hell.

INTRODUCTION

I was born and raised in Kentucky.

I got out when I could.

I visited when I could stand it, and when I couldn't stand being away another day, I moved back.

I have some family in Kentucky. I have deep roots in Kentucky. I also have a burial plot in a tasteful area of a tasteful, historic cemetery, a floral death-garden celebrating several centuries of gilded glory and marble-vaulted guilt.

Growing up amid the lace-trimmed graces of the Bluegrass was to be suffused with visual beauty and cultural richness.

It was Eden, but it was Eden after The Fall, haunted always by some notion of Original Sin.

(*Sex.*)

Parenthetical but ever-present.

Like most of our nation of hedonistic Puritans, the Kentucky in which I came of age could seem sex-infested, sex-infected, and sex-obsessed—terrified by the entire business of genital contact, the whole unsay-able drive to connect, in theory, in custom, and in horizontal practice. In any *genteel* conversation, just the *hint* of such matters, *sexual* matters, that key word with its three lingering syllables—*sex-u-al*—quickly compressed in a blushing Kentucky blur—*sex-shul*— was enough to produce fluster, bluster, shame and blame, followed by cloudy chaos and a frozen-faced laugh.

Or a dirty snort.

Or, and this most often, just a hollow silence.

Apprehension without comprehension.

"*Omne animal post coitum triste est.*"

(After sex, every animal is sad.)

That which is done but not discussed.

Enjoyed but not encouraged.

Denied, demanded, fulfilled, then again denied,
only to be pursued with renewed determination and
unassuaged fear.

And always *JUDGMENT*, capitalized, emphatic with
exclamation! Italicized by squirming guilt.

"The sins of the flesh."

Always, the *sins* of the flesh.

This is the Kentucky where I grew up:

Green when the rest of the country goes gray and brown.

White plank fences. Thoroughbred horses, beauty
unutterable, and privilege (for the few) unspeakable.

The ferny musk of boxwood.

African violets on kitchen windowsills.

Hens-and-Chicks, pale plant and succulent on
Mee-maw's front porch.

Sycamore trees stark against the winter-blue sky.

Mistletoe hanging high in the rotting walnut tree: the
kissing plant, always out of reach, always a parasite.

Southern.

Hulking old courthouses hoarding dusty records of
birth, marriage, discord, divorce, and death. *JUDGMENT* more
often than justice.

Old churches, mostly Protestant, molded along
the fierce lines of stony Calvinism. Steeples lifted, not in
aspiration, but in admonition. A smiting Hand lifted against
Its own creations.

Very Southern.

"'Revenge is mine,' saith the Lord."

The God who smiles on all this beauty and history
can be an icy Deity.

And it gets worse, or at least more complicated,
complication being the consequence of being human in a
social context.

As adults, my parents converted to Catholicism,
and I was raised Catholic. I was educated for twelve years in

Catholic schools by professional virgins, male and female, steadfast and stumbling.

The cultural ethos of my youth, however, remained stubbornly Protestant, deep-set in the legacies of the Puritans, the Baptists, the Evangelicals, and all the other cults that enjoy procreating, tout the sanctity of marriage, ballyhoo the moral superiority of heterosexuality, and preach relentlessly against those relentless sins of the flesh.

"Ah have sinned. O, Lordy, Lordy, Ah have sinned."

When we were children, we would pour over my mother's photograph albums, volume after volume of stop-motion joy.

"Say cheese!"

We always giggled over an especially cheesy picture, unlabeled and undated, of our Uncle Gene and Aunt Aleta, standing on a boat dock in their swimming clothes, their faces obscured in a tight embrace, the short woman's arms, not around the man's waist, but anchored hungrily about his neck, reeling him in for a deeper kiss. The only other place we would have seen that sort of embrace would have been in Hollywood movies on Saturday night television. Weepy love stories in black and white.

It was the way *actors* kissed.

Smooched.

Only this lip-locked picture was not made in Hollywood, but down on Herrington Lake, near Nicholasville, over in Jessamine County, near the high-climbing steps to Moore's Camp, post-war playground of the aspiring middle-class in Central Kentucky.

And—surprise! —the man and woman in the picture are *not* my uncle and aunt after all.

We called our father "Daddy Jack." In his later years, I told Daddy Jack how *funny* we had always found that photo of keen Gene and his eager wife. He looked puzzled. I found and showed him the photograph. "Oh, Kevin," he said, his Southern vowels pulled longer than usual by patient amusement, "that's a picture of me with your mother right after we got married."

Hearing of my ignorance, Mother hastened to label the old snapshot: "Annie and Jack." She used ink, her handwriting slanting sharply, firm and definite. "*Annie and Jack.*" She gave herself first-billing, but the "and" said it all.

Passion brushed bright with Pride.

Pride, however, was that commodity that "cometh before The Fall," and Kentucky seemed to graft shame to any display of pride. My parents made a few babies, but if Daddy Jack put his arm around Mother in our presence, she would slide, shift uncomfortably, push him away, and stretch out his name in warning: "Jaaaaaaaack!" Then a second time, with an upward inflection, "Jaaaaa-AAACK!" And then a third, quick, coldly curt with stinging consonants, "Ja*ck*! Don'*t*!"

Mother loved Daddy with the fervor of one who could never quite believe how entirely she was loved, but when we were near, she pushed him away. She had been *taught* what was appropriate in Kentucky. She lived by those lessons.

Time brought further complications to the branches of this tangled guilt.

My brother and I were—are—always *have been*—tenses be damned—both gay.

Born that way, as far as I can tell.

One day, when I was already past sixty, the *New York Times* told us that we now had to use the word "gay" and not "homosexual." Apparently, "homosexual" tends to make those who hear it think of those it attempts to describe as existing in a permanent state of sexual congress.

"Gay" is less horizontal.

I was brought up to respect the patriarchal lawgivers, and so I will honor the *New York Times*.

My brother and I *were* both homosexual. Now we are both gay, part of the expanding LGBTQ alphabet.

We are, of course, much more than that, but that is a *portion* of who we are. We are two brothers, each of whom is *also* a gay man.

"*And so, did you ever? Well, you know, did, like the two of you, you know, ever...?*"

"*Nuh-uh!*"

"*Never?*"

"*With my brother?*"

"*Yup.*"

"*Yuck.*"

Do straight men, heterosexual *guys*, have to endure questions about conjectured incest with their sisters?

Even in Kentucky?

My big brother has, however, always been my hero.

Each insecure, we handled our insecurities in different ways.

For my brother, being impeccable meant being irreproachable. He was always perfectly dressed, with never a smudge on his sleeve or a hole in his sock, nothing on his back that was purchased "on sale." A few years ago, I took him into a T. J. Maxx store; "What sort of place *is* this?" he marveled, as curious as Alice down a discount rabbit hole.

My ever-natty brother sought to float above malice and misconception. His perfection offered a form of isolation, the defense of a pristine distance. If there were nothing "wrong" to notice, he might feel invisible and, if invisible, then safe. As he entered middle-age, however, my brother found a new self-assurance. I knew this the first time I saw him in a pair of Dockers and an Old Navy tee. Ironed, of course.

I never cared much about how I looked or dressed, and it showed. I did like a hand-me-down, ripe-tomato-red sweater vest. I wore it until it nearly disintegrated into wooly pills. When puberty began its slow and secret siege, I coveted a green, three-piece, corduroy suit. I liked to be buttoned up and buttoned-down.

At thirteen, I tried to dress like an English teacher.

I memorized bits of poetry. At fourteen, I was mulling over Dickinson, Teasdale, and Millay, a dark feminine trio, but earlier, it had been the even-gloomier E. A. Poe.

From childhood's hour I have not been
As others were—I have not seen
As others saw…

I was eleven when I felt moved to commit these self-important lines to memory. The poem is called "Alone." I was scripting the first act of my self-drama. Even then I knew that I was indulging in a bit of a wallow, but words provided protection in order, solace in recognition, and retreat into artifice.

Rough translation: "Kick me!"

Bullied unmercifully, I also endured bad advice about how to survive at school. Mother, never Daddy, said I should hit back. I wasn't that stupid. Mother also coached me with snippy comebacks of the "sticks and stones" variety.

"Next time, why don't you just say…"

Stupid strategy: a provocation to further persecution, an explicit invitation to "break my bones." Fists fly faster than words. I was advised to keep my "chin up," and I did so.

Religiously.

At Sunday Mass, in our little church—small enough that you could feel your neighbor's Catholic nose poke into your face or back or backside with every move—I walked from our pew to the communion rail with my arms stiffly by my side. I was terrified that I was not "walking right." It is not as if I were tempted to twirl down the aisle like a ballet dancer *en pointe*, but I was afraid that the eyes of my classmates, their parents, and the "big kids" would judge my movement to be, somehow, in a way I could not define, not quite manly. So, I walked laboriously, with my nose tilted up to an unnatural angle. I thought I looked "dignified." I couldn't throw a football or dribble a basketball, but I worked hard to look *dignified*.

I had my priorities.

My eighth-grade teacher, Sister Alma Joseph, an old-school nun, swollen with piety and plump chins, presented me with a three-and-a-half-feet tall statue of Padua's St. Anthony, smooth cheeked and rouged. "I want Kevin to have Tony," she said. I took him home and put flowers at his sandaled feet. He was one of those chaste saints, pretty and untouched. I wonder now if I subconsciously found him "cute." Probably not. My prayers were as sexless as Tony's virginal legacy. Any carnal thoughts that were swimming in my hormones were drowned by my own search for sanctity; wannabe-saints should not contemplate the flesh, even flesh well-rouged in plaster. The statue disappeared somewhere in my parents' house when I was in college. Anthony, saint of lost items, was, himself, lost. By that time, at least according to the Catholic Church, so was I. "Tony" never reappeared. Neither did St. Kevin.

Being Catholic never simplifies matters.

Certainly not in Kentucky.

The Baptist God is inexorable and severe, but the Catholic God wields omnipresent clout, especially on the conscience and in the terrazzo-paved corridors of the bullied heart.

One compensates as best one can.

When we were in our early teens, I asked my nearly-perfect brother, "Why do we always think we are better than everybody else?" I was serious. I was concerned. I still wanted to be a saint.

With neither smile nor blink, my big brother explained, "Because we *are*."

We paused a moment to give that revelation its due. Then we laughed hysterically, swooping around in shrill giggles. We had a sense of the absurd.

How could we not? Absurdity was all around us.

The Kentucky town where I was born used to have a

small market on South Main called The Bluegrass Grocery with a motto on its plate-glass window:

"GOOD AS ANY, BETTER THAN SOME."

In my way, I have tried to live by that modestly-immodest motto. My memories usually support this presumption.

My big sister tells me that I remember too much, but memories are not facts. Facts get lost. Memories evolve. They insinuate and fuse. Memories endure, more or less, until they don't.

Time chips off the edges of fact.

Variations of Alzheimer's run in my family.

I have forgotten some specifics of time and place, but I go on remembering most feelings. They dwell just under my too-thin skin. If I misremember some details, it is because, somehow, I have to do so. Sometimes it is the memory, correct or incorrect, and not the fact that haunts me. I hope that I am not reckless, unfair, or unkind. I hope I am *dignified*, but I trust my nose is not "up in the air." I am not superior—just decidedly human, swimming against the current, and a bit tired. I have lived with the memories of my old bullies long enough to have developed a sort of numb acceptance of them, the memories *and* the bullies.

I have often tried to understand them. Both.

Sometimes I think I almost do.

Names appear in yearbooks, address books, on the backs of old photographs, or tombstones, but they are etched less steadily in memory. Names drop below the surface with time but float back up. Names honor the dead and the dying, the striving and the defeated. The real names that I use here I evoke with an affectionate clarity. The pseudonyms that I employ come with an ongoing attempt at emotional distance, protecting me, protecting *them*.

My tactful brother has urged me to "name the bitches," but I choose not to do so.

Calling out an old name that has meant pain is to court new pain.

And *Somebody-Somewhere* said, "Love thy enemy."

Biblical thinking presupposes that the world is peopled with enemies. Smiters are around to be forgiven, post-smiting. That's the "Christian" tradition, at least in theory.

I have been angry, although not, in the long run, with individuals, just about lost time and opportunities gone.

Usually.

Before he died, I asked my father, good as any and *much* better than most, if he had any life advice. What had he learned in his many years of experience with the human race? Daddy Jack smiled with his customary forbearance at my pompous request. "Oh, Kevin," he replied, "the Golden Rule. Most people are doing the best they can. Try not to judge."

I do try not to judge, but life lessons come from observation, comparisons of fresh dilemmas to old decisions. Choices follow this or that example. Metaphors strain to fit. Analogies help. If it manages not to cripple, experience is knowledge. William Blake distrusted experience as a loss of innocence, and innocence, like ignorance, is not really bliss, but oblivion.

In my life, however, I have met those whose words and actions seemed senseless, stupid, and cruel. If I seem to judge *them*, it is to survive them. Any unpleasant story I tell, I tell with as little animosity as I can manage. Anger fades. Experience lingers. Laughter helps. I know that my own blunders, cowardice, and selfishness have caused hurt, but calculated cruelty continues to anger me.

The manhandled topic of "sex" often makes me angry.

Invariably, of course, anger makes me ridiculous.

As I came of age in the Commonwealth of Kentucky, what I saw and heard and consequently surmised on the subject of sex accumulated in limestone layers of fantasy, terror, guilt, mystery, and chaos.

Sex has always been a messy topic. Ask Hamlet. Ask Hamlet's mother.

My mother advised me not to dwell in the past, but I can't help dwelling in my life. It is, so to speak, where I *live*. In truth, Mother never threw away a letter or a grudge. At times, however, when my feet are cold and I wake up in the middle of the night, I think too much of all that I should have forgotten. Stories return for rumination, like sour cud.

Emotional dyspepsia.

Acid reflux from the lower depths of the soul.

Sometimes these stories are with me at breakfast as I stare into my solo cup of tea. At times, they find me at noon in the middle of a busy day, and for years they have lingered in the twilight. Every evening the old vampires return. Mysteries, truths, and lies.

And so, a few of the lies I have told:

First Lie: "I am *bi*sexual."

Of course, what I meant when I temporarily staked my claim to bisexuality was, "I know I'm gay, and you know I know I'm gay, and I know that you know, but to make us all comfortable, we'll delay dealing with what we all know." I suspect I also meant, "I'm not what you call a *queer*! (Am I?)"

I have pretended to be confused when I wasn't, which was its own kind of confusion. I never, however, told anyone that I was a heterosexual.

Not even the women I slept with.

I apologize to all genuine bisexuals. I was not a good ambassador for that identity.

Second Lie: "I have forgiven the bullies who tormented me."

Only on a very busy day and never late at night.

Blanche Dubois said something about deliberate cruelty. You are welcome to look it up. She was a mess, in the way that only Southern literary creations can be a mess. I am, at least, a very literate Southerner.

Third Lie: "I don't hug people I just met."

I made my living for years in the theatre, lived in Manhattan, had West Side friends who went to East Side cocktail parties, counted Europeans among my friends, and got over it. Sometimes I even kiss both cheeks. *Mwah. Mwah.*

Fourth Lie: "I love you."

At least, I have never said it without believing that I meant it. It is possible to think you are telling the absolute truth and, all the while, be telling an absolute lie. As I have not yet fully figured out sex, it is unlikely that I have figured out love. Sex is a frantic mix of the physical and the emotional, but at least sex comes with a vague notion about what to touch. Love is less tangible and, anatomically, harder to locate. I have tried.

Heart? Head? Certainly not all genital, not all crotch.

Fifth Lie: "I am not afraid."

This is the best of lies and one that I intend to continue to tell myself.

I will, however, try to tell the truth here, the truth about the lies I was told about the evils of the flesh.

All that bad sex in Kentucky.

CHAPTER ONE

TWO HOMETOWNS

I have long lived a dual existence. As a working
actor, I was often myself by day and then, six
nights a week and at two matinees, some other person I was
paid to become. I was often on the road; home was a New
York studio and a series of bland hotels. Later I was a teacher,
"Mr. Dearinger" in the classroom and just "Kevin" at night.
As I began to write this, I was living in two homes, one in
Manhattan, a second in Kentucky. Now I have retired back
to Kentucky, but I still feel like a New Yorker, just as I was
Kentuckian in New York for four-and-a-half decades.

I am also, of course, a gay man living in a homophobic
world.

I am somewhat accustomed to this self-division, but
as I was growing up, time caught me between two hometowns and left me something of a stranger in each.

I was born in Versailles, perversely pronounced
"Vur-SALES." It was an intimate community. As Mother sat
up after the caesarian ordeal that produced me, she could
look out her hospital window and keep a maternal eye on
my brother and sister playing in our backyard on Douglas
Avenue.

Versailles loved gentle Annie. She knew nearly
everyone in town and nodded her head politely at the rest,
but Mother grew weary of being watched in Woodford
County. There is little privacy in a town where anyone

1

you meet feels free to call you "Honey" or "Sugar." Such familiarity gets sticky. And then one feels caught. Trapped.

We moved to Fayette County when I was four. Thirteen miles, as the crow flies. We'd be back. We stayed in our first house in Lexington for six days. Mother hated it. Wrong house in the *wrong* part of town. She would have none of it. We moved. Our second house had great neighbors, but too-little room for three too-noisy children. After six months, we moved again. The third house was home until I was in the third grade. Good yard, full basement, but small rooms. It would never have been a good home for three teenagers.

Lexington was not just a town. It was a respectable Southern *city*, with safely dead Confederates and secret vices in the dark, out behind the poolrooms, amid the tangled shrubbery of Woodland Park, on the sidewalks of the Esplanade, and under the battered streetlamps north of Main Street.

There were stories of Belle Brezing, notorious madam of a famously lavish whorehouse, with disenchanted mirrors, gas-lit chandeliers, and amber-tinted nights. She became a Kentucky legend, even if one not talked of in front of ladies. Belle had crumbled with time and died, with her mortal remains buried morally in the Catholic cemetery. Her house had also crumbled, burned, and been demolished, all on a street that marked the boundary between black and white.

For Lexington was a place of race.

Cheapside Park, where terrorized slaves once stood at public auction, lolled in its leafy shade. Grim-faced Confederates glowered from stone monuments. Solid high-ceilinged homes kept watch in stately old neighborhoods for Whites-Only.

(Dark-skinned "cleaning ladies" shaking rugs over the front porch rails, but only in the early morning when they were more-or-less unobserved.)

Sycamores and oaks and elms. Dogwoods in spring, and ginkgo trees, gold in autumn.

African Americans lived on the narrow streets of the North Side and old East End. Peeling frame houses and dirt yards. Howling dogs and coal stoves. Slamming screen doors and old folks silent on the porch.

Hackwood and honeysuckle. Disciplined rows of sturdy marigolds and astonished zinnias, hot-hued and proud.

There were no "black" suburbs to Lexington, but people of color lived *out in the country*, in "colored" communities where the road widened slightly for a quarter of a mile. *Little Georgetown. Little Texas.* Gray clapboard houses, brick churches with painted-glass windows, and maybe a grocery store. More front porches and screen doors. "Rainbo Bread." If you drove by, folks waved. If you slowed down or stopped, they slipped silently away.

Scrub cedars and spindly ash. Sunflowers and bindweed. Carefully-staked tomatoes and weed-less rows of beans and corn. Early potatoes turned up from the hot earth.

Caucasian shopping centers and, later, swan-white malls doomed downtown, leaving the urban African-Americans to a war zone of empty streets, dark offices, and deserted shops. Going-out-of-business signs stared into the street long after the businesses were gone.

Dying water-maples and broken lilacs. Wild chicory pushing pale and blue through the sidewalk cracks. A rebellious hollyhock.

Some of the elegant old movie theatres downtown had begun their lives as theatrical touring houses, real actors and all, but by the 1950s, dusty stages and abandoned dressing rooms languished behind faded silver-screens. Tarnished cupids, double-blinded by dust, slept on the peeling prosceniums, unmindful of what went on in the back rows of the dim auditoriums as the last of the B-movies played in triple-features. Randolph Scott and Ida Lupino, third-run Elvis, and finally Vincent Price.

"Scare the pants off you!"

By the time I was in college, most of the old theatres were parking lots. Daddy took us to protest marches in support of the preservation of the old downtown, but the bulldozers had more money. They always do.

Daddy Jack had grown up in Lexington and could point out where *things* happened. He showed us where he got tar on his good pants when he was seven. He showed us the short-cut alleys he later darted down on his morning paper route. He pointed out the nineteen houses he had lived in as a boy. The Great Depression and all that. A time when good, honest people could not pay their mortgage or their monthly rent, and so they moved from the grand house with the big porch, to the four-square residence, to the bungalow, to the cottage, to the low-slung shotgun house. Most folks, including all of my grandparents, both sides, blamed Herbert Hoover until they died and wouldn't have voted for a Republican if Jesus, or even the Reverend Billy Graham, had headed the G.O.P. ticket.

Then, when I was nine, we moved back into Woodford County, four miles from Versailles, nine miles from Lexington, between town and city, into a house of my parents' design. We called it "the country." We called it "the farm."

Five acres, with a barn, orchard, grape arbor, vast vegetable garden, tobacco allotment, a creek and a pond, wet-weather springs, seventy-two trees in the front yard, and a back pasture that rolled up and out to the eastern sky. Wild cherry climbing-trees and crawdad holes protected by towers of mud. Clear constellations high in the dark winter sky and galaxies of lightning bugs hovering in the summer humidity. A field intoxicated with wild mint. Frogs, heard but rarely seen, a quick plop in the water.

I was never a farm boy, but I knew every rock in the cold creek, every weed and flower in the field, and every bird's nest in every sheltered eave. I knew where the wasps would be, where the caterpillars would weave, and where the doodlebugs might hide. I knew the bank where the violets would first bloom each spring and which tree would hold its leaves longest as winter hunkered down.

"Going into town" now meant going back to Versailles. Population then 4,100, counting the Catholics, if you wanted to, but mostly Baptists, Methodists, Presbyterians, and generic "First Christians." Protestants with nothing left to protest except change and difference, and a stiff-starched clutch of meticulously-bleached Episcopalians who gave "teas." Catholics held card parties and "worshipped statues."

Black churches sang out on back streets or where the road dipped down toward the cemetery. "Afro-Methodist-Episcopal." *They* had "suppers." *Their* ladies went to church in go-to-hell hats and then directly to heaven.

On the edge of town, other churches had tent revivals, snake-handlers, and Sunday-night exhibitions of glossolalia.

"Come on down and be saved."

"P-raise! P-raise His-uh Hoooooly Name-uh."

"Et cum spiritu tuo."

"He is r-r-risen! He is r-r-risen, indeed-duh!"

On Sunday streets, rich ladies in black velvet hats with netted veils nodded in serene judgment, upper lips permanently lifted, as if trying with limited success to say the word "pencil."

(Try it.)

Two sisters, intellectual maiden ladies, lived above what had once been their father's dry goods store. As far as I knew, they were the only Jews in Versailles. I never met them, but they could be seen from time to time, peering out their high windows, from behind lace curtains.

Main Street had a quiet library with a special shelf behind the counter for adult-only books—*Peyton Place, Valley of the Dolls, The Carpetbaggers, Myra*

Breckinridge—and a corner drug store called The Corner Drug Store. If they sold condoms, I never saw them.

"Wha' ken I git furya?"

"Cherry Coke and a Milky Way, please."

"You one-a Anna Louise's boys?"

"Yes, ma'am."

"'Yes, ma'am!' Well now, lookee here, sugar, ain't you the little gentlemun!"

A noonday whistle, reliable and shrill. An iron-voiced clock-tower, water-fountains ("Whites Only") ("Colored Only"), and a courthouse with spittoons and overall-clad farmers; day laborers on the stone steps or leaning against the white brick walls in the hot sun, willing to be underpaid to bale hay in the midsummer heat. Soaked through with clean sweat by nine in the morning. Dirt-tired by sundown. Cash payment. No taxes. Enough for a few beers and a pack of cigarettes down at Wilson's Pool Room, with a little something to take home to the "old lady."

Barbershops run by men professionally silent and ironically balding. Customers waiting in stiff-backed chairs, killing time with nearly incomprehensible conversations, voices low, laconic, plodding on about sports, politics, difficult women, and hard labor. All in a vaguely misogynistic, talc-dusty haze. Dirty jokes left untold on the chance that a serious Baptist gentleman might be waiting, hat in hand, for a vacant chair and a trim.

The Farmer's Union, managed by steel-gray women, garrulous amid the scent of bluegrass seed and dried corn.

"Say 'scuse me' if you sneeze."

"Yes, ma'am."

"Jack Der-ner yer daddy?"

"Yes, ma'am."

"Mister Albert Lane yer gran-daddy?"

"Yes, ma'am."

"He the one used to farm over t' the Mason place?"

"Yes, ma'am."

"Un-huh, whud I thought."

"Yes, ma'am."

"Raised up right, I reckon."

Beauty Shops, the permeating smell of permanent waves and a blue haze of filtered cigarettes, with well-thumbed movie magazines by the dryers: "Dick and Liz and Liz and Dick." Sins of the flesh in Cinemascope. *Cleopatra.* Epic and obscene, with excessive eyeliner.

"Sandra, honey, be sure'n' spray that back part good and heavy so's it won't get all poochy."

"Any'uh you girls got an extra ciggy that's not some kinda nasty menthol?"

"Pass me that Screen Parade, *please, sugar, if it's new and don't smell too wet."*

"Well hello-Pete, I'm practically smokin' the filter!"

"Last week in Sunday school class I looked like I spent the night in a barn."

"Modern Screen's got that Marilyn Monroe again."

"Pass that ashtray this way if you're up and about, would ya?"

"Been dead a year or more'n that."

"And he spends all his money on something called Famous Monsters of Filmland."

"Uh-huh."

"Sounds like my no-good ex!"

"Uh-huh."

"Be grateful it's not Playboy, *honey. There's such that have to have that trash."*

"I saw somewhere that the Kennedys were in on it!"

"Shoo-wee!"

"Christine, this fool thing is burning the back of my neck! A-gain!"

"Now, honey, that's just right sad!"

"Uh-huh."

"What's this Ursula Andress woman supposed to have done that you know of?"

"She told me her hemorrhoids wuz yelping like dogs."

"She went outta here lookin' like a you-know-what to me."

"And don't cut off too much in the front like you did last time."

"And dropping off her like coconuts!"

"Mmm. Mmm. Mmm."

"Hammer-toed, and on both feet!"

"Well, there's pretty. And there's cheap."

"Uh-huh."

"If I wore those heels, I'd be laid-up for a month."

"Well, I swear to my goodness!"

"Mmm. Mmm. Mmm."

"Uh-huh."

The C&D Market, smelling of cinnamon and ground coffee, and The Bluegrass Grocery ("Good as any...").

Bessie's Bargain House on the edge of town. Bitter-cold, six-ounce bottles of Coca-Cola, Orange Crush, and Grapette. Heavy cans of Teen Queen Green Beans. ("Queenie Sez Yum!")

An old A&P with crowded shelves and gruesome meat counter.

And, of course, the Kroger Store.

"She can take you in her line, sugar, if yer cart ain't too full."

"Thank you, ma'am."

"You gonna use yer Top Value Stamps?"

"Yes, ma'am."

"You want that in a poke or you gunna carry hit by hitself?"

"In a bag, please, ma'am."

An actual Five-and Dime with Fizzies, Pez, Mallo-Cups, Red Hots, caramel cubes, candy cigarettes, and stale Tootsie-Rolls. Toys: Hasbro, Matchbox Cars, and Mattel ("Swell!"). Loom'n'Loops, everything you need to make colorful potholders for your grandmother. Or "One-hundred Toy Soldiers for One Dollar." Everything you need to start a war.

It was the America of Saturday morning television.

"Rock-em Sock-em Robots" scared me, but I found tactile comfort in the precision of "Lincoln Logs." Putting things together seemed better than "knockin' 'is block off." Early choices.

In cheery commercials between featured cartoons, I discovered a whole world of wants and needs.

Of course, not everything you wanted or needed was especially good for you. Kentucky was the land of tobacco and coal, and thereby the home-sweet-home of cancers various. In some parts of the state, coal put dinner on the table, even if the coal bosses ate better than their black-lunged workers.

Everyone smoked, or so it seemed. Smokers hacked and coughed. *Real* men cupped their cigarettes between thumb and index finger. *Ladies* twirled their ciggies at the tips of their index and middle fingers, flashes of lip-stick-smear on the filters.

If you got it wrong, used the wrong grip, someone noticed. Someone *judged*.

Smokers were branded by their brands. Parliaments gave you "extra margin," and the taste of a Kent defined "what happiness is." Bad boys crushed half-packs of Luckies or Camels, unfiltered, in the back pockets of their jeans.

"That first puff's always yer best."
"Stash one up behind yer ear for later."
"S alright, just flip the butt out the back-window."
"Them things'll kill ya, dead'r than a doornail."
"I know that. Lord knows, I know that."

Manly tobacco was still the primary local crop in the Bluegrass, having surpassed and replaced nineteenth-century hemp on the rolling farmland. Hemp still grew wild in the fields, and with some regularity a few adventurous proto-stoners would make themselves sick trying to smoke it, although it was only a weak cousin to the illegal cannabis.

"Like smoking yer sister's jump rope."
"Da-amn!"

9

Burley tobacco, however, was a government-regulated cash crop, beautiful in the field, majestic at harvest, and an art in its preparation for market. Cut-down and speared on worn wooden sticks, the stalks would hang for weeks in the vented barns to dry and cure, smelling of sweet dust and sticky leaf. Then, twisted into "hands" by the twisted hands of work-gnarled farmers, the leaves went to a noisy market where the auctioneer spoke like a deck of cards in full shuffle. Tobacco was "cured," but the end product of this delicate horticultural ritual was a medical scourge.

Even when allowed and allotted, Kentucky pleasures were tainted.

Blighted. Deadly.

"The wages of Sin."

And yet Versailles could be a friendly place. You spoke to everybody you passed on the street, even if you didn't know them, although you probably did. If you were in a car, you waved, or Mother tooted the horn. If a county road grew narrow, she would pull over and wave forward an oncoming car. The impulse of generosity was expected. Another kind of permanent wave.

If you didn't know someone, you probably knew something *about* them. Or you could guess by how they dressed. What they drove. How they walked. What brand they smoked. *How* they smoked. Whom they were with.

Teenagers, the white ones, circled around the parking lot at Dixie's Drive-In, swerved over to the Dairy Queen, or cruised up and down Main Street with full-blast radios.

"Here on the five-nine-o. Let WVLK start your day!"

"Juvenile delinquents in hotrods!"

"Yep."

"Da-doo-run-run-run. Da-doo-run-run."

"Just some trash from down on the river."

"Uh-huh, river-rats!

"Don't you ever let me catch you carrying on like that!"

"No, ma'am."

"Keep away from Run-around Sue."

"Somebody ought to call their preachers!"

"Somebody ought to call their mamas."

"Two, three, four! Tell the people what she wore."

"Oh, shoot, you know their daddies wur jes as bad!"

"She wore an itsy-bittsy, teeny-weeny, yellow polka dot bikini."

"You are listening to W-A-K-Y. Waaaacky radio."

Everyone knew someone who had been shot in a fight, someone cut up in a bar, someone in the "pokey," someone doing time in the "state pen, down 't Eddyville."

If you listened, you heard.

You *knew*.

Whispered stories that a first-cousin-once-removed had been arrested for driving fast, driving drunk, and driving in the nude.

"Nek-kid as a jay-bird."

He later found Jesus. Wrapped in swaddling clothes.

Jokes about the cuckolded husband coming home to find his wife in bed with a well-known county official. The randy politician, it was whispered, jumped out of the bedroom window and ran down the street. Without his clothes.

"Nek-kid as a jay-bird."

"In a subdivision?"

"Well, da-amn!"

But if he knew your daddy, he could erase a DUI, no real questions asked, no real money exchanged.

"Jesus H. Christ!"

Lexington and Versailles. My two hometowns in Kentucky, each historic with whispers, histrionic with stories only partially told.

In the Civil War of the mid-nineteenth century, Kentucky had been a border state, but a hundred years later, as I came of age, it remained a battlefield in another struggle, a cultural and moral war on human nature. Calvin's God has never seemed to approve of the natures He created.

Or maybe He just prefers the jay-birds.

If you listened, you learned.

Sex was "bad" in Kentucky.

And *yet*, if you listened hard enough, there was talk of something else.

In our first house, that wood-framed house in Versailles, Mother and Daddy Jack slept in a front room, facing Douglas Avenue. Their bedroom windows were gauzy with starched flounces of sheer curtains, like a perfect room in a Joan Crawford film. Or like a room *dressed* as Joan Crawford. Their mahogany bedroom set, "French Provincial," was still new, still unscratched, still being paid for in monthly installments. Their bed was a standard double, just big enough for two adults, and, on occasion, a scared child in flight from a nightmare. Mother's pillow smelled of Woodhue by Fabergé, Daddy's of soap and Colgate's. On the wall above their bed was a framed print of a placid Jesus, pointing with a Divine Index Finger to His Heart, open in His Chest, bleeding from wounds inflicted by jagged thorns.

"*The Sacred Heart.*"

The first word I associated with "heart" was "sacred."

The *heart* was sacred.

CHAPTER TWO

SUSIE AND ARTHUR, GRACIE AND JUNE

My father's mother's mother made her living selling sex.

That is not a speech exercise.

It is an awkward truth.

Susie, my great-grandmother, was the proprietress of a house of ill-repute. In fact, Susie ran a string of cathouses. Susie—a lady I never met but knew of as a *lady*, hair up, not always pretty in pictures, but aristocratic, even haughty, *dignified*, with enormous diamonds in her earlobes, thick body stiff in corsets under straining satin—was a hard-working, successful, full-fledged, high-bosomed, whorehouse madam.

In the pages of the old city directories from the 1890s, curdling on the public library shelf, Susie's name appears in the *business* section, along with an address on a notorious street in Lexington's old red-light district and her occupation: "MAD."

M-A-D. Madam. Belle Brezing's neighbor, her sororal competition.

Urban renewal has long since scoured away the actual street, but in the directory, it endures, for what it is worth. And *worth*, dollars and sensible cents, had been the reason for its creation, success, and longevity.

My brother and I had, in fact, first spotted Susie's name and its explanatory "MAD" when we were still in our teens, digging around in those same old directories. We liked libraries, shelves of consoling order and structure. It is a measure

of our innocence that we made absolutely nothing of that
"MAD." My brother, a dogged historian, finally deciphered
this code when we were both nearly as old as Susie was when
she died.

Susie's daughter, Gracie, my delicate grandmother,
gone now for over a quarter of a century, was tiny in stature
and tender in sensibility. She loved her husband, her children, her grandchildren, her piano, and her parents. If we
asked what she knew about her parents' early lives, she would
drawl politely, "Oh, honey, all that was a long time before *I*
came along." Then she would gaze off into the distance, silent
for a moment, and by the time her eyes returned to us, she
would have changed the subject to the present. My, but hadn't
we grown, and who would like a glass of iced tea or a choco-
late-stripe cookie?

"Might be a bit stale, honey, but still good."

It is only now that I realize what pain our curiosity must
have caused that gentle lady. Not that I think she understood
the concept of "shame" in any connection to her family, but
that she had been taught what was fitting to talk about and
what was not.

Gracie knew more, of course, than she could or
would reveal. There must have been the slurs at school,
even at the expensive schools or *especially* at the expensive
schools, and the whispers in the neighborhood. Kentucky
towns and Kentucky families have always been full of
whispers, whispers at school, at church, in the grocery, in
the drug store, in the hardware store, at the lumber yard,
rushing about the currents of life on Main Street, up the
tributaries of the residential streets, into over-heated
kitchens and under-heated bedrooms. A steady susurration
of scandal.

Susie ran a family business. She was assisted by Nettie
and Lil, two of her many sisters, all daughters of poverty,
women with no other course to turn to but the quilt-covered

bed up a narrow flight of stairs and the eiderdown of cash. They eventually left Lexington and set up "boarding houses" in Chattanooga, Montgomery, and who-knows-where else. Their shadowy trail is old now, difficult to follow or reconstruct. Their Kentucky brothers, steeped in the traditions of Southern honor and the necessity of hard labor, turned their heads, tilled their land, and tended their tills. Life was a struggle.

Do what you have to do and don't carry on about it. Go to church on Sundays and survive another week. His Eye is on the sparrow, but money puts food on the table. And money comes from hard work.

Gracie was born in Chattanooga. When her parents returned to live in Lexington, they brought their infant daughter; she grew up with puppies, canaries, and her own pony. Susie took up a sideline, raising prize-winning chickens. She contributed her advice to chicken-farmer magazines. "It was then," she wrote, "that I discovered that chickens must eat." Susie could be very practical. In Lexington, she prepared and served sandwiches and boiled eggs as part of the "free lunch" at her husband's saloon. She kept house and had a "girl come in to do the ironing," but now and then she left town to check on her "boarding houses." She remained a woman of business. Her energy was impressive. So was her determination to survive and thrive.

Domestic in Lexington, Susie read sentimental poetry, bought and *consulted* a massive encyclopedia, arranged flowers in gaudy-grand vases, and cooked so that her daughter did not have to. Susie's biscuits were legendary, but Gracie entered into matrimony with only one culinary skill. She made an excellent potato salad. For her husband and children, she would later learn to fry a fine chicken and deliciously overcook her green beans. Her kitchen smelled of Roman Meal Bread. She borrowed recipes from the women in her Sunday School class. She made a good bread pudding, mashed potatoes that stood up to a fork, and an onion-tomato-cucumber salad that was a benediction in the summer's heat. She made a sticky-sweet "worthy sauce" to be spooned over ice cream or cake, but she invariably made her coffee too strong. It was the only thing she ever made that was bitter.

When a very small child, my grandmother often stayed with her Aunt Nettie (*working woman, emeritus*) and Uncle Frank when her parents traveled out of town to check on Susie's financial ventures. Not quite asleep on a cot at the foot of their bed, Gracie heard her aunt and uncle talking about her parents. Their pillow talk was blunt. They said enough for my grandmother to know that all the Haviland in her mother's china cabinets, the mahogany furniture upholstered in green velvet, the claw-footed tables, the plaster bust of "Cleopatra," the portraits on matching brass easels, and the slate-roofed house itself, the high and grand house her parents had built in the *wrong* neighborhood of Lexington, were all the icing of respectability on a tainted cake.

When she could, Gracie "set a lovely table," an art she learned from Susie, but her mother's good china, cut-crystal, hand-painted platters, and rose-garnished bowls, were nearly all lost over the years, broken as my struggling grandparents moved from house to house to house during the Depression, or sold, piece by piece by piece, to a buyer remembered only as "The Mathews Woman," who showed up at the door with cash for one treasure and then another when the rent was due, the doctor had to be paid, or my grandfather was out of work.

Susie's necessary labor earned the cash that bought the luxuries that Gracie later sold for cash to pay for necessities.

In his youth, Susie's husband Arthur played semi-professional baseball. My great-grandfather was a good roller-skater, too; he knew a rough road when he was on it. In Lexington, he ran a saloon, a restaurant, a café, and a confectionary. None of his businesses were very successful, but he won a contest as the most popular man in town. The prize was a new car, which he promptly wrecked. There were complaints that someone had rigged the contest, allowing Arthur unfairly to beat out the closest competition, an especially adorable baby. Arthur raced trotting horses, and later he managed a respectable "family" vaudeville theatre on the courthouse square. Arthur was always adorable in his way.

A tale my grandmother told:

At first, Arthur encouraged little Gracie to play the piano and dance a bit on Thursday nights on the stage of his theatre. Eventually, however, he took his little girl aside, put a gentle arm around her shoulders, and said, "Baby, we've been letting you do this because you were cute, but now you're growing up, you're not as cute as you were, and you're not that good, so you won't be going on the stage anymore."

Gracie told this story again and again in middle and old age, but never bitterly, because "Baby" adored her father. "Baby" also had a very solid streak of common sense.

Gentle Gracie was never unkind, but she was often direct.

"Honey, I don't mean to pry, but…"

Life taught Gracie to face facts. Not always to talk about them, but to face them without a blink of her astonishing eyes. She did not wear glasses until she was in her eighties, and then it was only to read, at least until she forgot how to read. Growing up, she had known that she loved her music and her father, but that she was not destined for the stage. Her face in public might bring more talk, more gossip about Mama, whom she adored as she adored her father.

With huge bows tied in her hair and dresses ironed to crisp correctness by the "girl who came in," little Gracie attended several of Lexington's best private schools, but never for long periods. When times were hard, Arthur and

Susie sent their beloved daughter to the public schools, but, even there, Gracie's dresses remained crisp and her hair bows stylish. The "girl," of course, still came in to do the ironing, and Gracie's piano lessons continued. She practiced on an upright Chickering in the front parlor and prized the long chain of silver medals she won in recital competitions. When marriage, children, and Hoover's Depression wove worry and want into her life, she would still find money, somehow, somewhere, for piano, violin, and dancing lessons for her children. And those children were well-scrubbed, well-dressed, well-mannered, and got to school on time and to Church on Sunday.

But Gracie did not tell her children or her husband another fact of life she first suspected and then knew. She was an adopted child.

Loved. Adored. Adopted.

So were two of her female cousins, the daughters of Nettie and Lil, the two sisters who had, at least for a time, assisted in Susie's "business." The working-women of the sister-trio were not afraid of prostitution, but they were, it seems, terrified of child-bearing. Their mother had given birth to thirteen children, each destined to struggle for financial security. Worn out by childbirth, she had been old too early and dead too soon.

Three daughters, three cousins, were carried in the hearts if not in the wombs of three sisters. One cousin was made strong by her mother's past. She grew up in Texas and lived to be a hundred-and-two, a sharp-minded raconteuse to the end. The other cousin was gentle, somehow sad. When she was forty, her mother slapped her face for crossing her legs at the knees; no one knows how to be a lady better than the woman who isn't exactly one in the eyes of the town. That austere mother was a *lady* of the grandest sort; one would never have guessed that when she was a slip of a girl at twenty-nine, she had been arrested at a bawdy house on "drunk and disorderly" charges. She had demurely asked the police to wait a moment while she stepped back inside to retrieve some necessary item, only to return and offer herself up, stark naked, to the arresting officers.

"Nek-kid as a jay-bird."

During the worst of the Great Depression, Gracie, the eldest of the three cousins, made a home for her beloved husband, their five children, her father, her sister-in-law, and *her* husband. Twice-widowed, Gracie suffered loss, suffered love, stayed cheerful. In the haze of old age, her memories flew off into the wind like dandelion seed, and yet almost to the last, she could find her way to a keyboard and crash out the chords of the "Hungarian Rhapsodies." The Chickering was gone by then, replaced by a lighter spinet, suitable to modest, low-ceilinged *modern* housing, but the touch of the Chickering remained when other marks of grand living had disappeared, even as she began to forget names and repeat stories. Her comprehension of the world traveled in time, and even a trip down the basement steps became a testament of courage, but her back stayed straight. She perched on the edge of her chair, not allowing her delicate spine to touch the back support; she crossed her tiny feet tidily at the ankles and tucked them under her in a carefully rehearsed curve. Only in moments of self-conscious tomfoolery (and when Susie had been dead for half a century) would Gracie cross *her* legs at the knee, a comic show of spirited rebellion. The gesture, however, was never long in duration.

More of a *woman* than the law and conventional decency allowed, Susie raised Gracie to be a *lady* by society's strictest standards. Poverty in the Great Depression and, much later, dementia took their toll, but my grandmother's childhood training in harmonic resolution was ingrained. The last time I saw her, she was propped up in her bed, surrounded by stuffed animals and pretty-faced dolls, attempts to distract and comfort a mind that could neither focus nor be comforted. She had forgotten how to speak, but her lovely eyes followed me as I moved across the room. She wore an expression of expectation as if trying to remember once more the duties of a Kentucky hostess or the cherished rituals of a grandmother's love. Memory had fled. Courage and duty remained.

Susie's large family gave Gracie many other cousins, most of them remarkably unremarkable except in the way that all hardworking individuals are remarkable.

Some drank.

A few "ran around."

One turned tricks up until the eve of the Second World War. She stood in a small city park after dark, plying the family trade near a statue that celebrated the "Joy of Youth." If, as a child, my father pointed her out in the lamplight, his parents would shush and rush him past this wild-haired woman. She had been one of my grandmother's maids of honor. She had remained neither maidenly nor strictly honorable. Her parents sat at home, read their Bibles, grew weary, left a light on in the parlor, and went to bed, hoping their daughter would make it home. Some nights she did. Some nights she didn't.

And all the while uncoiled judgment hissed through the still nights of the then-small Southern town.

Gracie's father, my great-grandfather, Arthur was born a gentleman, a son of Georgia affluence. His father owned a popular bakery in Atlanta, the uneasy town that rose up from the ashes of war, the Atlanta of Margaret Mitchell and *Gone with the Wind*. His sisters married well, dressed for cocktails in the afternoon, and if they smoked, it was only at home and with cigarette holders. A less discreet rebel, Arthur paid a price for his indiscretions.

We *heard* that Arthur's first marriage ended when he discovered that his society wife was playing fast and loose with a lover. According to tales he told in a bathtub while my father scrubbed his back, Arthur strolled into a Chattanooga saloon and found his wife cavorting in the lap of her paramour. He pulled out a pistol and took aim, shooting out the gas flames in a chandelier, proving that he might easily have gunned them both down, had he so chosen. His wife's sniveling lover, he told my father, had waited three days and then, like a craven villain, ambushed him on the streets of Chattanooga, shooting him in the back. This explained the old man's bullet scars. My father rinsed the puckered skin in awe.

Such melodrama made a *good* story but not a particularly *true* story.

In truth, after his divorce from his first wife, Arthur had met Susie at her "house" in Chattanooga. Their devotion was deep, if not exclusive. Susie had her business, although by then she worked in the front office and not on the factory floor. Arthur also ran around with a local married woman. While squiring this woman on a surreptitious drive out along Missionary Ridge, Arthur was ambushed by the woman's husband and brother-in-law. As the assailants fired pistols out of the bracken, Arthur jumped from the buggy and ran for his life. They shot him in the back. The scars that my father would later scrub were not exactly honorable wounds by traditional standards. Well-known enough in Chattanooga to claim sanctuary, Arthur ran to the city jail and had himself locked up. No stranger herself to the police station, Susie visited him in his cell. They clung to each other "like innocent children," reported the local newspaper, until it came time for Susie to return "to her life of infamy." The *Police Gazette* reported the story nationally and sneered lewdly at the hapless "Southern Don Juan."

The Atlanta family disowned Arthur.

Or he disowned them.

He married Susie.

Or he did not marry Susie.

No marriage record has turned up.

Arthur and his first wife had a son, but "Papa" saw little of his blue-eyed offspring. At nineteen, the son's elopement with a sixteen-year-old girl from a prominent family rankled Atlanta as much as his parents' divorce had done. *Wild blood!*

After a month of marriage, his teenage bride discovered the affectionate letters he had received from the fallen flowers of Atlanta's whorehouses. Divorce followed. The boy, now a twenty-year-old man, became a reporter and covered the Spanish-America War.

My grandmother had a few vague memories of this *other* child, her half-brother. He visited Lexington from time to time in the first decade of the twentieth century. Susie loaned him money, and it all ended awkwardly. As did his life. "Oh," my grandmother would say with polite evasion, "he passed away a long, long time ago." Her tone was the one so often employed when social or sexual aberration called for a conversation that could not happen. Questions were not encouraged, and if asked, were left tactfully unaddressed. This was considered kindness.

During his brief marriage in Atlanta, my grandmother's half-brother fathered a son that no one in my immediate family even knew existed until a hundred-and-fifteen years later. What did *he* know? What was *he* told? What whispers did *he* hear?

And how, in defiance of good sense, had he ended up in New Jersey?

Eventually, Gracie married and gave birth to her five children, the eldest being my father. Still wary of childbirth, Susie hovered over her petite, pregnant daughter, but felled by a stroke, she died nine days before her first grandchild was born. Gracie grieved and then went upstairs to give birth to my father. She always boasted, modestly, that all of her children were born at home and that each tipped the scales at ten pounds or more. Tiny Gracie had robust children.

Or the doctor had a butcher's thumb.

Arthur lived out the rest of his life with his daughter and her family. In the white linen suit that marked his Atlanta upbringing, he would sit out on the front porch, commenting to the dog at his side on the passing parade of women, clicking along the sidewalk in nylons and high-heels, tight girdles, and lace-edged brassieres.

"Look at that hussy, Pal," he would say to the dog.

Good old Pal would wag his tail.

The *hussy* would wag hers.

Once, when he was in his seventies, Arthur went down into the Kentucky hills and brought back a mountain *girl* he said he intended to marry. My grandmother would not have complained, but she could not have approved. If nothing else, her house was already overcrowded, the budget strained. The girl did not stay long enough to become a woman or a wife. She quietly returned to Eastern Kentucky but left behind a blanket, a small memento of warmth that stayed in the house much longer than she did.

Gracie loved her husband without reservation. His name was June. If this struck anyone as a woman's name, no one ever mentioned it. Sometimes, he was June Bug. He later insisted that his given name was Julian, but my paternal grandfather was born in the month of June and was always called June.

June was born in Swallowfield, a tiny rural community just north of the Kentucky capital, in a house left unfinished when his grandfather died. My grandfather's grandfather was injured in the Civil War. A wound under one arm never quite healed. He wore a shawl because he could not comfortably wear a sleeve under that arm. He worked hard, lived close to the bone. When he died, many years after the end of the war, his wife collected a Confederate widow's pension. Several more generations lived in the unfinished house. When I was last in Swallowfield, it was still standing, if barely, supported by the spindly trees growing through its walls and floors and up its cramped staircase. Finished off, at last, by nature.

Many of the hard-working but somehow sullied men of June's family were carpenters. They appreciated that which was straight and square and sturdy. They guarded and maintained their beautiful saws, hammers, chisels, and the special tools-without-names that eased their labor and elevated their craft to an art. Carefully kept, the tools had to last, even as the bodies that employed them wore out with use and abuse.

A master carpenter himself, June kept everything in order. When my father was a bustling toddler and would not stand still while his father worked, June took off the boy's shoes, nailed them to the floor, and reinserted his first-born's tiny feet. Daddy learned patience.

When June was himself a child, his parents had taken him off to the wilds of Washington State, where they homesteaded, logged, further procreated, and aged prematurely. Restless, they relocated again to the plains of Alberta. They became Canadian citizens, developed some distinctly Western diphthongs, and then, leaving a married daughter behind, returned to Kentucky to reclaim U. S. citizenship. Back in Lexington, those prairie-honed sounds marked them out as somehow *peculiar*.

June's father, gaunt and weathered, played the violin, although he surely thought of it as a fiddle. When he died, his Kentucky comrades came to his funeral in tall white hoods and sheets. It was 1926, and American men of color were being lynched.

June heard the voices of racial hatred. He was perplexed, even horrified, perhaps with guilt. The n-word did not go unspoken in his presence. When they were courting, however, he wrote in a letter to Gracie that, surely "the Negroes" were "as much God's children" as they. Not much, perhaps, but an earthquake in Lexington in 1918.

He also wrote to tell her that he had heard unkind talk about her mother and father, whispers and sneers, but, he quickly explained, he still knew her parents to be "good folks." He did not see how it could be right to judge anyone by his parents. By *her* parents.

What June said would always be only a tiny portion of what he thought and felt. He *felt* deeply, but he had been raised to be a silent man, a man of the Northwest hills, a man of the Canadian plains, and man of Kentucky.

When he courted Gracie, June was living with his parents, less than two-hundred feet away from my grandmother's home, but he wrote to her almost daily. She would preserve his letters in her mother's massive steamer trunk long after Susie and June were gone and memory was going fast.

June wrote to the pretty girl down the street to say that someday, when he was successful, they would have a tidy bungalow in the country with a fenced-in garden and plenty of room for their children. He studied bookkeeping, but he had headaches, and in the end, he took up his father and grandfather's tools and built houses for the "rich bugs," south of Richmond Road. After they were married, he traveled to find work and wrote home to Gracie; he struggled with the "great big blue devils" of depression and longed to hold her just for a moment in his arms. He did what he could for his wife and "the Brats." As depression and The Depression caught at their souls, he reminded his Gracie, "You know by this time that we can stand darn most anything."

Later, June worked at Oak Ridge, knowing nothing of the plans there for an atomic bomb, but doing his part for the war effort. He craved high adventure but settled for hard labor. He grew tired but never complained.

After June's first heart attack, his doctor prescribed a diet of red meat. Gracie cooked massive steaks and roasts for him, still offering mayonnaise-rich potato salad on Sundays. He had a second heart attack. "This is the big one, boys," he told his cronies at the pool hall down on Limestone, and so it was. June was dead at fifty-seven, just like his father and his grandfather.

The Dearinger heart was sacred but scarred by genetics.

Gracie had headaches and heartaches. There were stories that June might have strayed from his marriage bed. If he lost something of his innocence, however, he always returned to Gracie, and she loved on, as was her nature. After his death, a woman appeared at Gracie's door to offer her personal condolences. My grandmother knew who the woman was and what that woman had tried to be to June. Gracious to the core but never a fool, Gracie shut the door with a delicate wrath. I wish I could remember who told me this story. Gracie would never have told such a tale on herself. Or on her beloved June.

Back before their marriage, June had written to Gracie with an impetuosity that he would later be too exhausted to feel. He wrote to her of love, of longing, and of lust, carefully phrased. They kissed and cuddled on her parents' front porch, behind the morning glory vines that offered some little shade in the long, hot August afternoons. The blossoms, sensing only the dark of their own density, would open in the early evening, with a delicacy so complete that if a hand brushed against their pink or purple, the sensation was only of color, never of substance. Like the love of two innocents.

June wrote to Gracie to meditate on their "sweet times" together. Their physical explorations pushed, *perhaps*, the limits of propriety, doing some of *what boys all wanted* and *no good girl should do*, following the urges that had moved generations before them to seek intimacy, to share bodies and caresses, and to feel the ecstasy of nature despite the Puritan blush of America. He yearned for her, he wrote, "as if my very soul is on fire with something I can hardly resist."

June hoped, and so he wrote to Gracie, that what

they were doing before marriage would not somehow hurt her or ruin the "sweetness" of the honeymoon for which they both longed. World War One has only recently ended. June's weak eyes and perhaps his family's Teutonic name, however softened by well over a century of American and Canadian life, had prevented his serving in the army, but when the war was over, he had heard all about the battles and all about syphilis. Downtown, in one of the smaller movie theatres, public-service films, offered in separate screenings for men and for women, warned of the ravages of what was then called "venereal disease." The doughboys had shouted, "Lafayette, we are here!" and the French had sent home the "French disease."

Gracie's parents were not convinced that June would ever be able to support their daughter as comfortably as they were certain she deserved. One way or the other, Susie and Arthur had been entrepreneurs. June was not. He read adventure stories and longed for the tall Western skies. He worked like a dog for his entire life, but he was a dreamer. As his passion for Gracie escalated during their courtship, however, he worried that her parents might suspect that he had held their sheltered child too close, too soon. Susie and Arthur, of course, possessed expert knowledge about the ways and waysides of sexual intimacy, but the young couple, even so desperately in love, would never have sought advice. "Baby" could not ask, and June, as a man, was supposed to just know these things.

But how?

Who was supposed to tell him anything?

Not his prairie-worn mother.

Not the old Kluxer with the fiddle.

In Lexington, Kentucky?

So much whispering.

A few dirty jokes.

And two young people, so much in love.

Kevin Lane Dearinger

Chapter Three

Ada and Albert

My maternal grandparents formed another love match, even if one composed of younger, even less experienced lovers than Gracie and June.

Albert Lane was one child of many, born to another craggy-faced Kentuckian, a farmer, and to another hard-working, soft-faced mother. He grew up near a Shaker village, a dying community of religious celibates.

When he was still in his teens, already long out of school, Albert left the Bluegrass to find work with a farmer in the western part of the state. Just as he stepped off the train in South Union, a buggy raced by him, a rig driven by a young woman with chestnut hair and a rod-straight back. She drove the team of horses with concentrated skill and fierce dignity. Albert was smitten. "That's the girl I am going to marry," he announced. When he arrived at his new employer's farm, he found out that the young woman in the buggy was the farmer's daughter. It was, of course, the stuff of legends.

That evening, he watched as the straight-backed beauty struggled to coerce a stubborn calf into a barn. Gallantly, he swept up the bleating animal and "tossed that little sucker in its stall," just for her.

By chiding coincidence, there was another Shaker village nearby. Albert, my story-telling grandfather, told us that the last religious celibates in the area once asked to adopt him. Had he been willing to foreswear sexual intimacy, he might have inherited rolling hills and rich farmland, or $83, 000—he always remembered the exact figure—when the colony at last collapsed. He had other plans. Tossing that calf into its pen in a display of teenage brawn, Albert had also tossed his heart into the ring.

My grandmother, Ada, pale-faced, with dark, delicately-arched eyebrows, was fifteen years old.

To be fair, she *thought* she was sixteen. Her mother died when she was two years old, and after that, no one bothered to track her age. Ada had no birth certificate and no memory of her mother, only a torn photograph to show her that the woman who died had been beautiful, had pierced ears, and, at least once, had been able to afford having her photograph taken. Ada's gaunt, high-waisted father remarried. She had two full sisters and several half-brothers. She had a few years of school, but at twelve she was sent to work at a railway hotel. She learned to be a generous cook and an immaculate housekeeper. She learned that if her hands ached after a long day's labor, holding them in cold water relieved the pain more efficiently than soaking them in warm water. Discomfort numbed, labor could continue.

When she was middle-aged, Ada sat down to write about her life, but after a page or two, she concluded that she was "too stupid" to describe her own experiences, a heart-rending conclusion. Closer to the truth, she was too busy living her life to write about it. Her mind was busy, but her hands were always busier—canning, cooking, cleaning, washing, sewing, crocheting, quilting. Introspection was for those with time to spare.

Like Gracie, Ada possessed faultless manners. She did not have the hovering, atoning parents who raised Gracie to be a "lady," but she looked around with a self-begotten pride of self. She knew how to set a table and fold a napkin. She said "Please" and "Thank you" and "Yes, ma'am." She also had the gumption, when circumstances required, to say, "No, sir!" and make it stick. ("Good as any, better than some.") Like Gracie, her back was straight. Unlike Gracie, Ada could drive a rig, churn butter, wring the neck of a chicken after breakfast and have the plucked poultry on the table for dinner at noon, but she, too, perched on the edge of her chair and crossed her ankles, never her knees.

And Albert fell in love.

So did she.

They were married for a very long time.

My grandfather Albert was patient until riled. Ada was gentle but rigid. She could nag. "Al-BERT! Uh, AL-bert." When he had a few drinks, she fumed, lower-lip set hard, dark eyebrows contracted in Biblical impatience. She was a life-long Baptist, worried that Catholics worshipped statues and wary of anyone with dark skin. Her own skin never saw the sun if she could help it. On a summer afternoon when she was a girl, helping her family move from one farm to another, she had fallen asleep on the top of a wagonload of furniture and nearly died of sunstroke. In her nineties, her pale shoulders remained as milky-smooth as those of a fifteen-year-old, severely-Caucasian bride.

Albert took up farming, and Ada "took up housekeeping." There were no children right away, and Ada recalled how lonesome she felt when, housework finished, she sat in the silent farmhouse while Albert worked out in the fields. She remembered that by midafternoon she would regularly set out to find him; he always stopped what he was doing to hug her and kiss her until she felt better.

After a few years of marriage, the babies started coming, and they came regularly for twenty-five years. The twins died, one at birth and another within the month. The tiny clothes of the dead were packed away, soft with the smell of baby powder. There were a number of miscarriages, not spoken of, defying utterance. The last to come, when Ada was well into her forties, was stillborn. Six of her infants survived, however, each unfolding in life as a complicated reaction to its parents, emulating and rejecting the traits and chosen habits of Ada and Albert Lane. All of their children were remarkably stubborn, each quick to feel a slight, each passionate: internal fires, covered at times but never extinguished. Late in life, Ada would tell a granddaughter who was determined to "keep her figure" that the best physical exercise was a good love life. "All the Lane men," added my grandmother, in a confiding tone, were "warm-hearted."

Baptists have a way with euphemisms.

Mother remembered that her parents often laughed together. When I knew them in their middle and late years, they were still laughing. They "tickled" and teased each other with private jokes.

When their house burned down in the mid-Fifties, Ada and Albert stayed with us for a few months, sharing the room I shared with my brother. My brother and I slept together in a single child's bed. Ada and Albert spooned each night in its twin. Ada and Albert did not complain.

When he was in his nineties, however, Albert set up a bed in a spare room. My grandmother later explained this arrangement to me. She snored. Albert would nap in the second room until she had quieted in her sleep, and then he would creep back beside her in the high double bed they shared. With pride, she told me that he never spent a full night in the spare room.

And, she said, he continued to keep her company after his death. "I haven't had a single night since your grand-daddy passed away," she declared with a cryptic smile, "that he hasn't come to me in my dreams."

Ada would survive Albert by eight years.

When Albert drank, his warm Lane heart would beat a bit faster. He became grabby and kissy. If we were around, Ada would push him away, but she would giggle. Nevertheless, she joined the Women's Temperance Union and carried in her purse the WTU pledge to not partake of, serve, or allow intoxicating spirits in her home. At least once, according to one of my cousins, she thumped Albert on the head with an enameled saucepan when he came home tipsy.

Having abandoned thoughts of writing her life's story, for a time Ada used her diary to keep brief notes on visiting company, her "practical" nursing work, and Albert's trips to the poolroom. "Albert's been drinking," she once wrote in steady ink. Several days later, she recorded, "Mr. Lane is *drunk*." The next night she wrote hastily with a blunt pencil, "The old man is soused!"

Albert was a strong man, even about his weaknesses, and one day he decided to stop drinking and smoking. And so he did. He was in his sixties. Ada still kept her WTU card in her purse, along with a box of Bible verses on small colored cards. She kept Albert in her bed, and then in her dreams.

Ada could be judgmental about women who "carried on" with men, but she usually found a gracious forgiveness for transgressions of the amorous sort. She could amend her prejudices. She once told me she liked a lady friend of mine who happened to be African-American, but in her next breath she earnestly warned me that she would rather see me "dead" at her "feet" than "married to a black woman." When she was older, however, she seemed to change her views on race. She counted her neighbors of color among her most treasured, and when she was felled by a stroke and suffered the interminable hell of "long-term care," she shared a room with a nearly comatose African-American woman. Unable herself to hear well, see well, speak, or walk, Ada fretted about the well-being of her moaning roommate. Nearly helpless, my grandmother would send me with a gesture or a look to check on the even more helpless woman across the room.

It's too bad that Baptists don't believe in Purgatory. I

like to think that Ada's misery in "long-term care" somehow purified her life, counterbalancing her human faults.

We were always close, but I was fascinated by what I did not understand about my grandmother. I was also terrified by what I imagined she might know about me. I would have been mortified had she had ever thought I was not the best little boy in the world, but to my consternation, she often told me that she liked "bad little boys best." She would say that she only lived into old age that she might see my children, the "gran'babies" I was supposed to begin to beget. I knew early on that was not likely to happen. It was not possible to explain to her that I was not likely to marry a black woman or, for that matter, any woman. I wonder now if telling her I was gay might have made me one of the "bad little boys" she prized.

Probably not.

My grandmother loved me, no question, but she was a Baptist, no argument. In those days, in that place, *liberal* Baptists were a rare species.

Albert was a good, good man, but perhaps his bit of "bad" kept their love alive. Sex was never spoken of, but my mother's parents shared an intimacy that was intense, body and soul.

Chapter Four

Jack and Annie

"What you have to understand, Kevin," my father told me when he was older and I was old enough, "is that I love your mother."

Daddy Jack was a college professor, a civil engineer who wrote fine poetry and built fine furniture. When he was away overnight on academic business, Mother would bring out his framed photograph, taken when they were courting and inscribed, "To Annie, with all my love, Jack." She would put the photo on her bedside table. Just before he returned home, she would tuck it back in a drawer.

Once, when he seemed a bit worn down, I told Daddy of the photograph that came and went as he left and returned. He knew all about it.

Loving Mother allowed him to understand her. Or, perhaps, the other way around.

By the time we were teenagers, Daddy Jack was a warm and wise presence in our lives, but early on, if my memories are true, he could seem remote, a bit gruff. "Grouchy" was the word I used in my early journals. Daddy was overworked and fretted about his delicate wife. "Annie," he wrote to her, just before I was born, "I know I am not perfect but please let me know what I can do to make you happier."

Early on, Mother subscribed to the "wait until your father gets home" approach to child discipline. She might "swat a behind" in the heat of the moment, but Daddy Jack was the one sent to spank us. A leather belt on the back of the legs. Not often. Terrible for all. Later, if the old spankings came up in a family anecdote, Daddy's voice would crack, and tears would well up in his eyes.

When I did not want to move up in scouting, from Cub to Webelos to Boy Scout, Mother was the one who was *really* furious, but I knew that I had let Daddy down. He put up a basketball hoop and gave us basketballs and footballs, but I preferred my puppet shows. One year I got a punching bag for Christmas; at first, I was afraid that it might hit me back and then I was just bored with it. Daddy set up an archery target and let us practice with a bow he had carved himself when he was a boy, but I turned back to my books. He read, too, but he liked to go fishing. Fishing seemed dull to me. Daddy's old tackle box became my first theatrical make-up box. He liked to go camping in the woods, and I liked that, too, but I was happy to get home to the television. Good man that he was, he earned the right to be "grouchy" from time to time.

Daddy Jack cooed over us with playful nicknames and punny jokes. He would make a dive for our tender bellies and tickle us "silly." On long Sunday drives, he recited from memory the poems of Robert W. Service, "The Shooting of Dan McGrew" and "The Cremation of Sam McGee." Then we'd stop on Jefferson Street for French-Bauer, the "best ice cream in the world." Mother always had a dish of strawberry.

Daddy also read to us.
The Five-hundred Hats of Bartholomew Cubbins
Hans Brinker and the Silver Skates
Tom Sawyer
Huckleberry Finn
Treasure Island
I was sure that Daddy Jack had somehow once

been Jim Hawkins and personally known Long John Silver. Perhaps he had.

He read Dickens to us.

Oliver Twist

David Copperfield

And short stories:

"The Birds." Scarier than the movie.

"By the Waters of Babylon." Puzzling and sad.

"There Will Come Soft Rains." Terrifyingly possible.

We were fascinated by variations of Armageddon.

We also loved humor, and all the more when what seemed funny to us might not seem funny to our peers. We, my brother and I especially, liked to think that we harbored some secret and protective knowledge. Chuckling along, Daddy read to us:

"The Secret Life of Walter Mitty"

"The Night the Bed Fell on Father"

"The Bear Who Could Take It or Leave It Alone"

Daddy loved James Thurber, and so we loved James Thurber.

He still read to us when we were in high school.

He also introduced us to Shakespeare, Poe, Burroughs (Edgar Rice), Teasdale, Millay, *Fantasia* and *Bullwinkle*, *Oklahoma* and *The Music Man*.

He sang in a small, true tenor voice. Sentimental ballads, hymns, a few show tunes, and campfire ditties:

"Once I Went a-Swimmin'"

"The Bear Went Over the Mountain"

"Row, Row, Row, Your Boat"

"Freres Jacques"

"I've Been to the Animal Fair."

He made us laugh, and we sang along, tethering our lives to music.

Daddy Jack knew how to put a comforting hand on a small shoulder. If we cried, he made silly jokes that made our tears seem beside the point. When I got my first low grade on a report card, Daddy searched around in the attic and found his own fifth-grade report. As an adult, he was a skilled mathematician, but he, too, had initially struggled with fractions.

When Daddy told us that he loved us, we knew without question that he did. Whatever love is, it must be what he felt for Mother and felt for us. He loved without ever resorting to recriminations. His love encouraged us to learn from mistakes, to grow, move on, refrain from judgment, and love in the manner that was most natural.

Mother sang, too, but quietly, when she thought she was alone. She crooned, scooping like Bing Crosby, connecting the notes with dips and dives. Her voice, heard from another room, could break my heart.

"The Red River Valley"

"True Love"

"Fascination"

"How Can Our Love Be Wrong?"

"People Will Say We're In Love"

"Smoke Gets in Your Eyes"

And always, "Always."

Mother loved us, too, with storybook tenderness. Her love took the form of perpetual worry and a hovering fuss over her three children.

My earliest memory: *She peers down at me in my crib. Her dark hair tumbles forward around an unlined face. Tender-voiced and softly Southern, she says my name. Her love is a whisper over my head, freshly-laundered baby clothes, and a blanket tucked in around my toes.*

This memory may be from the time that I had pneumonia and nearly died. I was eighteen months old. I had been a plump, healthy baby, but after this illness, I was spindly and coddled as "sickly" for a number of years. Mother always insisted that I could not possibly remember any of this time, but I remember her long hair. She cut her hair short before I was two, a severe cut that survived as her style for the rest of her life.

One of Mother's hairdressers, a very short gay man, would later perm and tease the front of her hair into Baptist-lady heights, but the hair on the back of Mother's head remained cropped, butchered close, like a penitent nun, or a prisoner of the Inquisition. Seriously-Catholic hair. Maria Falconetti in the flames of martyrdom.

Mother claimed that she could not bear the feel of her hair tickling the back of her neck. It made her "nervous." American life in the Fifties and Sixties resounded with endless talk of "nerves." Ambitious decades, always on the edge.

"My nerves are not good."

"My nerves are shot."

"I'm feeling kind of shaky."

"I'm so nervous I might come out of my skin."

"The Wasteland" lived out in Kentucky.

(Overheard and terrifying: *"Kevin is a nervous child."*)

Mother was pretty, and yet she seemed to make herself less attractive, less feminine. *Harder* under a protective shell.

She was not always hard-shelled. She had been the kind one, the gentle one, the middle daughter who gave her family quiet devotion, but even as a teenager, she had a stubborn streak. Her older brother called her "Caldonia," after a popular song lyric about a hard-headed woman. She grew up stubborn in a house filled with stubborn people. As she got older, Mother found it more and more difficult to accept the shortcomings of her siblings, her mother, her neighbors, her co-workers, her husband, and her children. Throughout her life, Mother idealized those she loved, only to discover their human flaws. Each time, love seemed to drag her deeper into disillusion and distrust. She could not reconcile her feathered expectations with leaden reality. Her stubbornness battled with her intrinsic gentleness, and the conflict caused her great pain. Each year, she developed an increasingly sharp and wounding defensive edge that too easily felt and gave offense. Her self-protective reflexes were as bewildering to her as to us.

I find her in myself.

In *official* photos, posed and poised in youth, Mother looks like Ingrid Bergman. What's more, she looks like she *knows* that she looks like Ingrid Bergman. She smiles a movie star smile, what we used to call "the schneer," a dazzling display of teeth produced after a sharp intake of breath. *Schhhh.* She would take off her glasses and brace herself for the camera. Our family albums and home movies are full of "the schneer." For our childhood photos, we three, the children, conjured up our own version of that smile. We learned when it was time to peel back the upper lip and show the teeth. As adults, we tend to face a camera with tight lips and frantic eyes.

Mother shrewdly edited her photo albums and home movies, eliminating images that she imagined made her "look like Mrs. Roosevelt." Eleanor Roosevelt was a grand and admirable woman, but she was not Ingrid Bergman.

In the albums and home movies of our aunts and uncles, Mother also appears, glasses in one hand and cigarette in the other, with "the schneer" broadening her face into a shining display-case of cheery confidence.

From time to time, however, Mother is visible in the background of photographs taken without her knowledge. In these images, she wears her glasses and a frightened frown. Her hands fumble up nervously to touch her face, to hide her thoughts. She looks lost. When I remember this look from life, it is against my will. It's of a piece with that sad music of her singing in another room. Tragic and helpless. That look became her day-to-day face, haunted and confused. Hurt and distrustful. Beyond comfort.

Daddy knew the look.

"What you have to remember, Kevin, is that I love

your mother."

It is hard to imagine that Daddy ever discussed the logistics of love and sex with his exhausted father, although June might have warned him against venereal disease. The army would have repeated that warning. In marriage with Mother, it would have been unnecessary knowledge.

I suppose.

Am I naïve in suspecting that my parents both came to their honeymoon as virgins? Am I really even allowed to speculate on the subject? I certainly never asked them about *that.*

Daddy had gone off to "the last good war" as a more or less engaged man. During basic training, he confided to his diary that after a few drinks with his buddies, he "looked over the local supply of streetwalkers," but headed back to the barracks "before being tempted too much." The war in Europe was more about death than desire, but as the conflict wound down to its last days and he waited to be shipped back home, Daddy was "beleaguered," his term, by female attention in France. A handsome army officer with a gentle manner would have been attractive to an unattached mademoiselle, or madam, made poor by invasion.

Daddy had a "girl back home." She dumped him and later married one of his best friends. He never seemed bothered by this. Mother joked that she got him "on the rebound," but there is *that* photograph of them, after a swim in the lake, standing in a tight embrace, the Hollywood clinch *du jour*. Did they learn of love at the movies? That kiss is passionate.

Mother had been hotly pursued by several young farm boys. One of them tried to give her a red convertible, an offer she virtuously declined. When she and Daddy ran into this old flame sixty years later in a Kroger's parking lot, he recognized Mother immediately and opened his wallet to prove that he carried her picture with him and always had. His wife waited in a hardtop car, ready to go home to something more sensible than young love.

Did they, Mother and Daddy, together or with some other earlier love, go further than a kiss? How far and how early?

None of my business.

None of anyone's business.

Tasteful not to ask.

Sensible not to wonder.

If, like most of my generation, I have trouble imagining my parents having sex after marriage, I find it impossible to conjure up any image of premarital "canoodling," again Daddy's word.

Perhaps they needed to wait.

Mother broke off their first engagement, and Daddy, in frustration, hurled the returned engagement ring out into the vast lawn that fronted Mother's childhood home. Nearly seventy years later, Mother would still dismiss his gesture as "silly." A second engagement led to a wedding, simple and small, in an austere but elegant chapel. A wobbly soprano warbled "Because…God Made Thee Mine" and "Oh, Promise Me." Mother wore a small brimmed hat and a white suit, sensible and tailored to show her petite figure. But definitely white.

For many years, the exact location of my parents' honeymoon was their shared secret. They also shared traditional standards of morality, and each possessed a personal sense of what was fitting. They shared poetry. Just for Daddy, Mother read Mrs. Browning.

"And, if God choose, I shall but love thee better after death."

What could Mother have known before marriage about the "facts of life" and the mechanics of procreation?

She grew up on a farm. She knew about cows and bulls, hens and roosters, mares and stallions, nanny-goats and bucking billy-goats, but it is easy to imagine that she averted her eyes and asked no questions. Ada did not tell her much of anything. She was busy tending house, raising chickens, cooking three enormous meals a day, and having babies. Mother told me that they never had "the talk." Maybe Ada thought that the logistics were obvious. She knew that Anna Louise evaluated the world with a quick mind. Always more self-reliant than she thought she was, Mother remembered learning about sex "the hard way," from friends, a few books full of evasion and euphemism, and what she overheard when adults thought she was "out of listening range." Her "hard way" to sex education was the *usual* way for generations of Kentuckians. Whatever Mother overheard as a child, when the grownups talked about the "delicate" subject, would have been too delicate to be practical. When she picked up a "balloon" on the road and a family friend shrieked at her to drop "that dirty thing" at once, she could only wonder if everything on the road, rocks included, must be "dirty." No one explained a "condom" to her. Such things did not exist in the Baptist world.

There was a man who lived on the farm with them who was rumored to be a genius and to have been around the world; he also beat his wife from time to time. Hunkered down in the bushes by the creek, he drew naked women with some flair of artistic talent and a suggestion of intimate knowledge. Mother remembered how oddly this made her feel.

When she was in the eighth grade, Mother noticed that her school-bus driver would regularly stop at a house on a bend of a county road, adjust his hat in the rearview mirror, leave the school children in their seats, and step into the house to pay a call on the mother of one of his young charges. After a time, the driver would reappear, readjust his hat, and continue his rounds. A few years later, he began to stop for visits with that mother's daughter. He still adjusted his hat before and afterward, just so.

During her high school years, Mother worked at Foley's, a small grocery "in town," in Versailles, a few doors up Main Street from a store-front funeral parlor. The undertaker was married, but he also had a long-term lady friend, a woman known only as Blue Heaven. Blue Heaven paid afternoon visits to her mortician-lover at his establishment. Or so Mother heard. And should the undertaker's prim wife happen to amble in the direction of Main Street, the downtown regulars would send a warning ahead, lest her straying spouse be taken un-aware. On these occasions, the undertaker would greet his wife at the parlor door with uxorious geniality. All the while, Blue Heaven lay quiet, hidden in a display coffin, resting, not in eternal peace, but only until the coast was clear.

Love and Death.

Small-town *Liebestod*.

Mother was never stupid. She knew the goings-on in Versailles. She always seemed to have heard who was stepping out with whom and on whom. It later helped that her big sister ran a beauty parlor, but nearly every evening, when I was growing up, there was at least one phone call so long of duration and so secret of content that it necessitated a cup of coffee, a cigarette, the snatching off of an earring, and the shush-shushing away of children. Versailles could certainly talk, and it always seemed to call Mother just after supper. She was steady, reliable, and good for sensible advice.

She also had a "private line" for her telephone when "party lines" still flourished.

Mother was discreet. She took in secrets and kept them. She was a good listener, but who listened to her? Daddy tried, but she had her secrets from him. Not *facts*, just *feelings* that she somehow could not communicate to him or anybody. Mother hated crowds. In crowds, she was most lonely.

Bad Sex in Kentucky

By middle-age, Mother's closest friends were nuns and priests. Celibates. She advised them. They advised her. Some of them were intelligent, strong, and sweetly good, but in some, the sacred hearts were seriously damaged. Screwy celibates. With this mixed lot of virgins, Mother sought a spiritual life to soothe her troubled soul. She called one egomaniacal, controlling ex-Jesuit-turned-Trappist her "spiritual husband," which I found creepy and intolerable, but which Daddy appears to have accepted. Or understood. Or endured. This religious demagogue hovered hatefully to the political right of Attila the Hun, even as his more modest religious brothers were answering the call of the social conscience and liberal spirit of the times. His fears of the fabled "sins of the flesh" were soul-destroying. The soul he infected was my mother's. I am bothered that he seemed to wish to take her away from us, but his greater sin was his campaign to take her away from herself.

And why, I have to wonder, would a man or a woman ever choose celibacy? Religious fervor is an oft-cited and, at times, genuine explanation, but fear seems to lurk as a contributing factor. Treating sexual attraction as a "distraction" is rather like announcing that legs are in the way of walking. Being "married to Christ" is a dodgy metaphor for defining a nature-defying choice. I suspect that Bernini got it right with the *Ecstasy of St. Teresa*. Sexual pleasure, even when suppressed, may be more closely aligned with the soul and the spirit than religion would have us believe. I am always slightly shocked by the erotic lyrics of sacred songs.

> *Jesus, Jesus, come to me.*
> *All my longing is for Thee.*
> *Of all friends the best Thou art.*
> *Make of me Thy counterpart.*

A few years before Daddy Jack died, he and Mother brought a rather irritating friend to my Lexington home. They had given me their old double bed, part of that mahogany set that they bought on a time plan at Montgomery-Ward when they first married. "Well, Kevin," smirked this obnoxious visitor, "how does it feel to sleep in the bed you were conceived in?"

I gave the question the silence it deserved.

Under his breath, Daddy whispered to me, "Presumptuous woman!"

On a June day of Daddy's last summer, I met my parents for lunch. I had my camera and asked if I might take their picture. Daddy put his arm around Mother, and, at last, she did not flinch or pull away, even with my presence and with a camera recording the moment. Instead, she dropped her head in trust on his shoulder. She smiled, almost with a giggle, like her mother's, and with nothing of the "schneer." I took the picture, and there it is, in the photograph, *marital bliss,* hard-won, eternal, my parents, lover and beloved, each of them home at last.

I was fifty-four years old.

CHAPTER FIVE

THE AUNTS

If with something more than modesty, Mother seemed to hide her Bergman beauty—and it was certainly beauty—the aunts seemed to be all lipstick and libido. There were five of them, Mother's older and younger sisters, and Daddy's three younger sisters. Most of them seemed to marry early and often. Counting remarriages to a previous spouse, at least once with another husband in between, the five women went, roughly, through twenty wedding ceremonies. Mother and Daddy married once. Only one uncle had more than one wife.

Aunts were exotic. They had *experience*.

Mother's oldest sister was the "great and good Christine," Daddy's description. As a girl, Aunt Chris ignored once too often her mother's warnings not to flop down on the edge of her bed. My mother, of course, never *flopped*, but her big sister made it a habit. And so, Aunt Chris finally flopped once too often on the high soft mattress, forgetting that she had left a sewing needle on the bed. The needle was still in her backside when she died in her nineties. For years she was certain that the embedded metal might somehow work its way up to her heart and kill her. Again, the sacred heart endarted.

Aunt Chris had a lovely, soft and round face, but her heart was always "full" or "hurt" or "beating *so* fast, honey, I can feel it." Her eyes, however, could go steely when she needed to stare down reality.

47

She was a hard-working businesswoman, a hairdresser, exhausted from standing all day on her feet and by late afternoon ready for a sweet iced tea, a filter-tipped Old Gold, and a good talk. She could talk because she had heard it all. When my female cousins wanted the facts of life, free from Protestant protestations, they would go to Aunt Chris.

Kentucky's answer to Chaucer's "Wife of Bath," Aunt Chris had four husbands and a child by each of the first three. Husband One died young; she always insisted that her final resting spot would be by his side, and so it was, nearly seventy years later. Husband Two was a wild-blood, tragically brilliant and unreliable, charming as hell, and hell to live with. Husband Three had some early fame as a local Lothario and dandy. He nearly missed the birth of their son because he could not get his hat to look just right on his head before going to the hospital. By the time I was aware of him, he just looked exhausted, but he had apparently forsaken his career as a great lover when he married Aunt Chris. He had been christened Clarence, but with the Kentucky insistence that real men sport manly names, he was called "Bootie." Only in Kentucky, the land of Buddy and Bubba, would sharing a name with a baby's knitted footwear be considered manly. Emphasis was, of course, on the "boot."

Once, while my parents vacationed in Europe, our family's affectionate border collie, Lady, stayed with Aunt Chris and Uncle Bootie. Aunt Chris, who penned sentimental poetry and dramatic letters, wrote to tell me that she had been awakened from a sound sleep in the middle of the night by the sensuous warmth of heavy breathing on her neck. "Kevin, honey," she wrote, "I thought it was Old Bootie feeling his oats after all these years." I think she was disappointed that what she took for rekindled passion was only a collie dog needing to go outside for a pee at three in the morning.

Aunt Chris always appreciated a frisky man. A frisky dog, not so much.

In her only big church wedding, Aunt Chris wed Husband Four on the day after her eighty-sixth birthday. She was a beautiful bride, dressed in pale blue satin, her still-tender feet made glamorous by gilded slippers. The wedding car, a hulking, low-riding sedan, decked out with the traditional old shoes and tin cans, sported a handicap tag.

Aunt Chris survived kind-hearted Husband Four by about a year. In her casket, the ninety-year old woman looked sixty at most, her hair coiffed and combed, her makeup perfect. Her daughter Donna, the lusty by-product of Husband Two, announced with teary pride, that her mom looked like Mae West.

She did.

I got Ingrid Bergman. Donna got Mae West.

Donna looked perplexed, however, when she heard of her mother's frank conversations with her nieces on the topic of sex. Apparently, Aunt Chris was a circumspect Baptist with her own children, even if she was outspoken with her nieces.

With her nephews, she was cushy and cozy, a soft-hugging aunt who would snuggle and say, "Give me some sugar, honey. Give me some *sugar*."

It was clear that she liked men. Aside from her husbands, to whom she was scrupulously faithful, Aunt Chris enjoyed *looking* at men. "Hon-neeeee," she would marvel, when a brash young man would hulk into her vicinity, "he is sooooo good-looking!" She loved the salesmen who came to her shop and flirted. They never got anywhere, but the flirtation was a good game for a game girl.

What did she tell the "girl" cousins? It took me years to ask, but eventually, I did. Aunt Chris was a far better source of information on menstrual cycles, pregnancy woes, and the greater and lesser points of the male anatomy than a junior-high slumber party.

At a family wedding, my female cousins and my

sister found themselves embroiled in a discussion on the subject of age and female pubic hair. They knew, of course, only one authority to settle the question. The "girls" called Aunt Chris. My sister, having moved from youthful shyness to a fearless maturity, asked her bluntly enough, "Aunt Chris, when you get old, does your puss turn gray?" Aunt Chris tee-heed for a moment, tucked the telephone receiver familiarly under her chin, and being a licensed beautician, addressed this question of hair down there.

"Well sure, honey," she said, "if there's any left."

Always discreet, she refused to cite her sources or admit personal experience on the topic.

Aunt Chris was always good for a good story. She was convinced that E. T., Spielberg's gentle extraterrestrial, was the anti-Christ. "If that E. T. showed up on my back porch," she said to me over a glass of iced tea, "I'd kill it with a skillet."

She was a natural poet.

Aunt Chris wasn't at first sure how she was supposed to react when a beloved granddaughter married a Muslim gentleman, but she figured it out. "*They* pronounce it "Mooooslim," she told me, and she became a fierce defender of Muslim-American rights.

Blood was thicker than prejudice.

When the 1960s rolled in, Aunt Chris, hairdresser and woman, took a professional dislike to any man with long hair. The crease between her eyes would deepen in disapproval. "Looks like a girl," she would declare. "Like a girl," of course, meant "gay," but that was not a word she had at her disposal and not a word she would have used if she had. She had harsher words, and I suspect she used them. Everyone her age used them when the kids weren't around, and sometimes when they were. "Queer." Like most of the women in her family, she liked a "good little bad boy," and as I remained determined every day to be an entirely "good boy," I was perplexed, even as I loved her.

Her sister Minnie, my mother's baby sister, played softball. "Fast Pitch," the hard kind. She played with fierce expertise and ended up with well-earned honors and a commemorative plaque in the Kentucky Softball Hall of Fame. Like my mother, she often wore her hair cropped close to her head, and like her sister Christine, she wore a great slash of lipstick, even on the ball field. She endured a blurry tumble of marriages. When she was married to Husband Three, a tough-talking cigar smoker who at times had to be smoked out of the pool halls late at night, she was at her athletic peak. She was on a team of spirited Good Ol' Girls, amateur ballplayers but dedicated to winning, self-motivated, even if coached and managed by men. They posed "tough," and some of them were what my mother would have called "rough." Some of the women, like my aunt, juggled jobs and motherhood to find time to play. A number of them never married, *very* tough women, not interested in playing girly-girl games, but they all adored Minnie, the defender of third base and the pro on the pitcher's mound.

Aunt Minnie, under her sturdy pose as tender and affectionate as a puppy, had an especially tough friend called Jerrie. She was one of quite a few Kentucky women with names like Billie, Charlie, and Jackie, the –ie alterations still sporting the five o'clock shadow of their masculine origin. "Rough and tough."

We would go on hot summer nights to Woodland Park to watch Aunt Minnie play under the harsh lights of the ball field. She was a star out there in the dirt, the dust, and the sweat. Feet firm in the earth, shoulders squared in concentration, eyes squinted in fine focus, and bright red mouth set, with a small twist to the right. The grass was a super-saturated green that stretched beyond the edges of the artificial illumination into dark, forbidding shadows.

Only later would I hear whispers of what went on in the leafy shade and black of night. Woodland Park had been notorious since before the Great War and remained so for long after.

Aunt Minnie enjoyed a good time. When she had a drink, she, like her father, became amorous, *handsy* under alcohol. She also got *nippy*. She would grab my good-little-boy toes and play "This little piggy." She was being friendly, but when "this little piggy said 'wee, wee, wee' all the way home," she would twist my tender little toe like a female Grand Inquisitor. And the *coup de grâce*: she would kiss me all over my neck and face, leaving great red lipstick smears, as if marking me in some ancient rite of passage. Perhaps she was. Like Aunt Chris, Aunt Minnie would ask for "sugar," but with Aunt Minnie, it might come back to you in lumps.

I liked her.

I loved her, as I did all my aunts.

She was far from delicate and could be remarkably abrupt, direct, uncensored, unfiltered, all the things that, in my insecurity, I feared, but she, too, seemed a bit lost, uncomfortable at times, confined, uneasy with limitations, troubled by expectations. She called herself a "big ol' tomboy," a "Daddy's Girl." She was happier in "slacks" than a dress. She referred to her long-held job with the state government as a membership in the "K. M. A. Club." The initials represented a jocular vulgarity, and she delivered this bon mot with a no-harm-done guffaw.

After she retired, ever restless, Aunt Minnie traveled around the world, here and there and everywhere. She took long cruises. She sat on sandy beaches. She got lost in Russia and rescued herself. She stood in the ruins of the Parthenon, washed her feet in the waters of Jericho, walked the Great Wall of China, rode to the top of the Eiffel Tower, and was visiting Rome "when they shot the Pope." She was unable to keep still in one place. She always regretted not riding on a camel in Morocco.

In old age, her eyes softened into the misty blue patience of her father's, but she could not pretend patience with the rigors of infirmity. Driven by the stubbornness that marked all her kindred, she stared down old age, scowled at its indignities, and dared it to cross the line. Her life had moments of soul-breaking tragedy, but if she felt a moment of self-pity, it never showed.

Oh, for the glory of one more no-hitter!

"Love you, Aunt Minnie," I would say. "Love you, too, sugar," she'd reply, fearless even in the presence of sudden sentimentality, not knowing that in *her* presence I still involuntarily curled my toes in self-protection and unaware that I was grateful for the example of her powerful eccentricity.

Daddy's sisters were an entirely different breed of aunts, but they, too, wore an air of bright lights and glamour. In maturity, each sported a head of slightly-improbable red hair, ranging in shades from deep auburn, cut sleekly to frame the face, to Lucille-Ball-henna in a furious fluff.

The youngest, Ruth, was dramatic, in life and even more so on the stages of the local community theatres. She was a good actress and had a good heart. She also had three husbands: a mercurial Irishman with wobbly dentures, a rather credulous younger man who never quite realized that she had children nearly his age, and a convivial man who wore black tee-shirts and took her to pubs and cocktail lounges. She trusted anyone and everyone. She was often cheated and even robbed by those she protected, but she never complained or backed away from her generosity. She never learned to drive. She smoked when she shouldn't and wore bright yellow because she could. She floated on a sea of helpless strength.

Aunt Loralie, the middle sister, was a dancer. She kept her dancer's discipline well into her senior years, faithfully doing her time at the barre, keeping her waist trim and her spine erect. She was utterly feminine, almost girly, in her flirty ways. She did a memorable imitation of Evelyn Keyes as Suellen, Scarlett O'Hara's whiny sister, but she would have made a better Scarlett; like Scarlett, she would have been willing to dance all night and into the dawn. Aunt Loralie had a prim demeanor and a raucous laugh. She saw no need to suffer fools and didn't.

She had style, *great* style, with open eyes and open heart, and she never put a *paper* napkin on her table. "If you watch the sales," she advised, "you can always keep up a good supply of nice linen napkins." She once came to my home for tea—tea was *dignified*. My cups and saucers were a hodge-podge of mismatched glass, ceramic, and cracked china pieces. "Oh," said Aunt Loralie, eyeing the lone and lovely Haviland cup and saucer, "I'll have *that* one."

Aunt Loralie married a dashing man from California. He was not only handsome, but he played tennis, manifestly the mark of a superior gentleman; to Kentuckians, California was golden. So was Uncle Jim.

When she visited from California, Loralie disrupted all traces of Kentucky torpidity. She seemed to be everywhere, laughing, opinionated, inquisitive, supportive, and alive. When she was back home in Pasadena, she sent letters and cards that sputtered and spun with exclamation marks and underscored emphasis. She lived every day with the same staggering energy. Her tiny Pasadena garden erupted with California color, a celebration of Loralie's impatient soul. Like Aunt Chris, she wrote poetry. Like her mother Gracie, she was tiny. When she drove her red Triumph TR3 on the L. A. Freeway, her eyes peeked not over but *through* the steering wheel. From behind, the sporty roadster appeared to be driving itself, fast, daring, and determined, weaving in and out of traffic. "*Mrs.* Toad's Wild Ride," she called it. Her almost-dangerous force never quite found its full outlet, but she tried, she tried, she tried. Aunt

Loralie was never bored, never boring. To have been either would have been a waste of her time, a waste of her dancer's precision, her measured steps and startling leaps.

The eldest of my paternal aunts, Aunt Sue eventually had the brightest tints in her red hair, but she was the shyest of the three sisters. Daddy always said she was the "really smart one" in the family. "Pick of the litter," he would add, with loving irreverence.

My aunt escaped a sad early marriage by joining the WAVES, and, in the midst of war, found delirious joy in the strong arms and deep voice of a heart-stoppingly handsome man from Oklahoma. He was the love of her life. Her young beauty alongside his movie-star head, chiseled and manly, made them an unforgettable couple, a work of visual art. There was a delicacy to her movement, a grace to her company, that announced her happiness with him. They laughed together in a low, contented rumble.

Aunt Sue was gentle, easily hurt, rarely complaining. Particularly in front of her adoring nephews and nieces, she pushed down any sadness with a ready wit and a weakness for puns. She never asked for "sugar," but she was reassuringly tender. She never addressed me, or my siblings or my cousins, as if we were disreputable house-pets. She spoke to us as she spoke to her sons, as if we were a wondrous part of the world that she loved. She spoke of nature, novels, plays, music, poetry, and politics. Her usual manner was Southern-slow, intelligent with patient *knowing*, but social issues could make her rage. She fought all forms of injustice and was a proud Liberal of the Kennedy sort. She stood in vigils to protest wars and capital punishment. She spoke up to protect forests, small animals, old houses, the rights of women, and the dignity of veterans. She also played the piano and sang show tunes and romantic ballads. She listened to Barbra Streisand when no one else in Kentucky knew who the singer was going to become.

Aunt Sue divorced the Oklahoma man.

She never said why, but she always regretted it, and when that marriage ended, something broke in her and in the entire family, on all sides. None of us really survived without a wound. Her brilliant sons gathered all the light they could still find and held it deep in their artists' souls. For all of us, marriage suddenly seemed a terrifying contract with no guarantees, no safety nets, and no second chances. If *this* marriage could end, what union could possibly last? If you lost a great love, could any other love replace it?

Aunt Sue married twice more, each time in good faith and with affection, but the man from Oklahoma remained in her soul.

Stupidly, I went to her estate sale. An older man with unconvincing hair had been hired to organize the sad event. I heard him bray to a bargain hunter, "Oh, the lady who lived here was *glamorous*, a real Auntie Mame, with red hair and lots of it." He seemed to reduce my aunt's gentle life to a show and a spectacle. "She was more than that," I said in a sharper tone than I had planned. I stood by a table of her turquoise jewelry, near a stack of her sheet music, and by a pile of old Streisand albums. "She was smart and funny, kind and good."

Heartbroken by love given and love taken.

CHAPTER SIX

KISSING COUSINS

I seem to have skipped most of my uncles. They usually skipped me. One had tattoos, and several told racist-sexist jokes in "funny" voices. A few ruffled my hair and asked what sports I played. When I proved unable to discuss athletics with them, conversation ceased. Most were quiet in the way that dusty tombs are quiet. Perhaps they were loquacious around their own children, but on the occasions when they ran into a nephew, they were too tired to make small talk beyond the usual masculine grunts. They aimed at stoic; they settled for comatose. Such was the manner of Kentucky manhood. Usually silent and somehow nearly sullen.

Most of the male cousins were much the same. When we were all small, we might be begrudging playmates on a Sunday afternoon while our parents drank dark coffee and smoked, but with puberty came silence and retreat. A few of them impregnated their first semi-serious, semi-adult, semi-conscious girlfriends. Sometimes a hastily-announced Saturday afternoon wedding followed, with a reception in the church hall, before adjourning to the divorce court nine months later. Daddy and I represented our branch of the family at a blur of ceremonies where we met the bride for the first time at the reception and never saw her again.

One cousin went to Viet Nam and nearly died for all our sins. We heard the adults whisper that he had survived "shrapnel in the groin." It wasn't the groin. "Hell," he said, a bit too loudly at a family funeral, many years later, "don't you know they shot my balls off in 'Nam." I heard him and remembered my well-meaning participation in anti-war marches in college. He was *over there when I wasn't*, and he came back with injuries no one could talk about.

Some of the younger male cousins took up drugs without thought and grunge without style. Some found Jesus. Some found happiness. Some found happiness *and* Jesus. Some fell into the Republican Party. Some I barely knew or know. By the early Seventies, our families were all adrift.

My "girl" cousins were quite another matter. Some were boisterous, but even the shyer ones vibrated with edgy inquiry. They came of age amid the urgent outcry for women's rights. They insisted on the social freedoms that their mothers had only found in clandestine clutches, marriages, divorces, marriages, divorces, settlements, custody battles, and mellowing age. They practiced kissing with cousins ("Whoops!") and danced the "Wooly Bully" (*"Matty told Hatty, 'bout a thang she saw..."*). They sought in vain for sexual enlightenment in the underground lyrics of "Louie, Louie." They listened to the Stones and "The House of the Rising Sun," the reputed "ruin of many a poor boy." They argued over which Beatle was the cutest and whispered rumors that Ringo was "a queer."

(I tried to figure out what this meant. Did rings on his fingers mark him as "queer?")

My female cousins watched their generation rush into a rash of early marriages, with all the whispers of "a have-to case" and "preggers" following some quick run-away ceremony. Instant husband and wife, a highway motel, and back home the next day to murmured congratulations that smothered the sniggering contempt, each couple treated as if they were the first in history that had not waited until the knot was tied to unwrap the package.

"The bride did not wear white."

Then began the numbering of the months, like a dancer counting a choreographed routine, five-six-seven-eight, and never quite reaching nine.

There were alternatives.

In the days before Roe vs. Wade, there were stories about doctors who "would do *it*" and, even more terrifying, stories of the "coat hanger." When a soap-opera character had daytime television's first abortion, doors were shut all over Kentucky to allow the womenfolk to mull over the dark details. My sister told her younger brothers what she knew about it, but we understood almost nothing of it. Another "it."

We all knew someone, however, who ended up at the Crittenton Home for "unwed mothers" with its fenced yard and privacy hedges in a bad neighborhood. No one ever went there officially, openly, publicly.

"She had to go away for a while."
"She's visiting friends out of state."
"Oh, she got the mono bad. Real bad."

Babies were "given up" and never heard of again. Philip Larkin described the "shame that comes at sixteen." For the Kentucky girl who "gave in" and was then forced to "give up," the effects of shame could come earlier but live long into middle age.

So much loss.

With time, it became socially acceptable to be a "birth mother." Phil Donahue helped. Oprah guided. Graying women who had not been allowed to be young mothers sought out the children who had been theirs for only nine months and a few minutes.

Another story overheard, piecemeal, in adult whispers:

In the 1960s, a popular high school quarterback impregnated a nice local girl. The boy's Baptist parents watched as their son's teammates lined up at the office of the county judge, each testifying that they, too, had "known" the girl. "In the Biblical sense." This was before DNA testing. The judge proclaimed the girl a "public whore," and the Baptist boy went on his way, legally childless, blameless in his social and religious circles.

Then the girl did the unheard of. She did *not* leave town. She stayed on. The baby was born. The teenaged mother rolled her chubby-cheeked innocent up and down Main Street in a second-hand stroller. A pioneer, proud to be a public "birth mother." The older generation shrank away from her. The younger women watched in wonder.

"O, brave new world!"

In this culture, my "girl" cousins improvised their roles as lovers and mothers and wives. As individuals. Most of the older ones were probably wedding-night virgins, the younger ones not so much so. The ones who got out of Kentucky danced more freely on larger stages. One is an artist, soft in speech and bold in color. One is a choreographer and producer, a force for the performing arts. Another retired early to sail a boat around the Caribbean with a spouse and faithful dog. One was asked years ago to pose for *Playboy*; her father vetoed the proposal in a voice of patriarchal thunder. Still, we thought in admiration, she had been *asked*.

The women who stayed on in Kentucky lived with strength, but their ears and souls could only have wearied at the admonishing clucks heard on Main Street and in the cramped churches. They endured. Several shed husbands like wooly layers of itchy winter clothing. One is a successful business entrepreneur. A few have been "born again," in the established religious sense of the phrase. At fifty-something, one is a grandmother and weekend "biker chick." Her middle-aged cleavage is a frequent flyer on Facebook. These women, my cousins, were and are, each and every one, astonishing survivors.

Many of these cousins joined the great Women's March of 2017. Magnificent in their pink-pussy hats, their faces enriched by experience, these women glowed with an inextinguishable passion for justice, a glorious beauty. They well remembered the old days and had no intention of going back there or of allowing their granddaughters to suffer the patriarchal fools they had been forced to endure.

I have spent a lifetime pondering my family.

I think I love them.

My mind keeps working to lodge Love and Understanding in adjoining brain cells, with connecting doors. Daddy did this better than I can, but I try.

When I was in my thirties, my friend Joyce, an elderly English actress, heaved her ample bosom and spoke of me. She kept her consonants crisp, knowing I could not help but overhear her. "Oh, Kev's alright," she said, "unless he starts talking about that fucking family of his in Kentucky."

Dear old Joyce may have been right in her RADA way. I have spent years turning over my thoughts and telling stories about my relatives. Her use of the blush-inducing participle seems particularly appropriate: sex made vulgar in Kentucky. But we, the eff-ing family, have mostly survived and been happy.

Mostly.

And I say, well, good for us.

Sorry about the F-Word, Mother.

Kevin Lane Dearinger

CHAPTER SEVEN

CATHOLIC SCHOOLS: AN ELEMENTARY EDUCATION

Being Catholic in a primarily Protestant state was not easy, although the discomfort was assuaged by the level of ridiculousness that compounded Kentucky sexual mores with the dictates of a celibate prelate in Rome.

It helps to be able to laugh.

I was expelled from a papist kindergarten.

When I heard that all the other kids were already five, I rebelled against the demand that I go to school. I was only *four*. Had I waited from September to November, I would have been five, but emotion trumped rudimentary mathematics. I wanted to be back home with my mother. I had enjoyed her daytime company exclusively for a full year as my big brother and big sister trotted off to school, but Mother had taken a job, and now I had mine. I was told to loosen my hold on "the apron strings."

Instead, I fiercely clutched what I could.

About two weeks in, I tore the kindergarten nun's rosary to bits, bead by bead. I intended no harm. My big sister had a plastic pop-bead necklace, high fashion in her third-grade set, and I was sure that my teacher's rosary might also be snapped apart and easily popped back together. Good in theory, not so in practice. Shocked by my sacrilege, Sister Rita Marie locked me in the cloakroom and summoned the monsignor to "drive out the demons" in me. This is another event that Mother always insisted never happened, but my memory of this occasion is concrete. Absolute. This threat of exorcism *happened*. I remember the not-so-good priest looming over me with his red face, disdainful scowl, piggy eyes, and hard-domed baldness: a penis wearing bifocals. I hid under the bookshelf *under* my school desk. The space could not have been more than seven inches high. I was that small, that wiry, that determined, and that frightened.

At four, I had already seen the face of Satan.

Our first house, the wood-frame on Douglas Avenue, had a large, grated, hot air vent in the middle of the dining room floor. Poor design. My brother had crawled onto it and been slightly burned. My father built a low, white picket fence around the grate to protect us. Good design. Good parent. A picket fence, of course, was the post-war symbol of domestic security, but I had my terrors. The fire below had somehow hurt my brother. When I was still three years old, I dreamed that I was wandering in tunnels beneath our house towards the source of a burning heat, the fiery furnace, hell. My sister was with me, her yellow hair rendered by my subconscious as scrambled eggs. We were aware that something else was in the tunnels, something that could harm us. We felt its hot breath. It was the devil. He was near and getting nearer.

So, I cowered under my kindergarten desk because I recognized the thundering monsignor. He was the demon of my nightmare tunnels.

I was expelled from the fruitless Eden of pre-school and sent home in shame.

My sweet paternal grandmother volunteered to stay with me. Unfortunately for this arrangement, she brought along my sour step-grandfather.

Gracie had only recently abbreviated her widowhood by marrying this "good Christian" widower from down the street. Gus taught Adult Sunday School. He had searched his Bible and bracketed every scriptural passage mandating the subjugation of wives to their husbands. Some passages were vigorously underlined and embellished with exclamatory punctuation. Gus was blustering and brusque and everything I mistrusted of grim masculinity.

On my first day home in disgrace, I looked out the front door and saw my grandmother and scowling Gus coming up the sidewalk. Fearing the demons that the monsignor had conjured, not dislodged, I locked them out of the house, front and kitchen doors. It wasn't, of course, sweet Gracie who scared me. It was Gus. Barking orders, he growled at me through the door and then skulked, head-down and fierce, around the side of the house, scurrying to the basement door. I was faster and got down the stairs in time to lock that door, too. A standoff followed. Pleas from my grandmother; threats from Gus. Eventually, the lady next door, a woman I worshipped, talked me into unlocking the doors.

Her name was Ersal.

Only in Kentucky is a name like Ersal possible.

Ersal had a son who "was a movie star," and like Aunt Chris, Ersal was a hairdresser. She laughed often and loud and always seemed happy. She made Mother laugh. She made us all laugh. She was an *adventure*. She fussed over me and cooed over the color of my sometime-red hair. In fact, most often, cut short in a manly "burr," my fuzzy head was sun-bleached to white, what used to be called "tow-headed."

I was a very pale child.

For a time, when I was four and five, I would slip through the unlocked back door of Ersal's house when no one was home and sit for hours in the crowded closet of her front bedroom. The smell of mothballs amid the rack of soft winter coats was comforting. What I liked best, however, was the quiet darkness.

Around this time, something had gone wrong in our own house.

Mother was on uneasy terms with her "nerves." Even as children, we regularly heard of someone, usually a female relative with several small offspring, having a "nervous breakdown," but we heard stories that June, my hardworking paternal grandfather, had also suffered a "breakdown," when his parents died, first one and then quickly the other.

Mother had at least two such breaks.

Emotional fractures.

Cracks in the smooth surface she worked so hard to keep intact.

Mother was scared of storms, afraid to be alone at night when Daddy had to travel or came in late from work. She read books about "emotional loving" and underlined the passages that spoke to her. She had headaches and took afternoon naps in a darkened room. From any place in the house, I learned to recognize the fizz of two tablets of Alka-Selzer in a glass of water.

"Try not to bother your mommy right now."

As long as I was small enough, Mother would wash my hair in the kitchen sink. She would arrange a towel on the countertop. I would stretch out, squirmy, and she would gently work the shampoo into my hair and then rinse out the suds with the kitchen sink spray, checking first that the water was neither too cold nor too hot, then towel my head tenderly, scoop me up, and place me on the floor. Gently.

Mother's hands were soft, but sometimes they shook.

Once, just once, I heard Mother and Daddy argue. Daddy's low, placating murmur, his words uncatchable from the next room. Mother, sharp and distinct, hurling terrible words, words I did not want to hear. Her normally soft Southern voice strained and broke, hard and hurt. "I go into the bathroom," she shouted, "and wipe my face with my washcloth, and you've used it to wipe your *butt*."

We were not allowed to say the word "butt."

We had backsides and sat on our *bee-hinds*.

As this argument escalated, Mother threw a saucer at Daddy. The yellow Fiestaware struck the matching-yellow kitchen wall at just about my height, near the door to the dining room. In the comic strip "Bringing Up Father," harridan Maggie regularly hurled plates and vases at the head of Jiggs, her harried husband. *This* fight, however, was not in the funny-papers, and Mother was not a harridan. She was still "Mommy" but suddenly unrecognizable. I was in the next room when it happened, but I knew that had I been standing *there* and not around the corner, the saucer would have struck my face. I imagined this injury until it seemed as if it had happened. It hadn't, but another had. There was a hole in the kitchen wall. Daddy patched it with plaster, but a hatch-scored scar remained a permanent trauma.

Mother and Daddy loved us, loved each other. This was certain then. It remains certain now. And Mother was as unlikely to be physically violent as Daddy. Her gentle soul was bewildered. So was Daddy's. Until we left that house for good, however, the sight of that patched wall filled me with a shame I could not understand.

In family photographs, we all smiled broadly.

"The schneer."

Repaired plaster.

Only later did Mother tell me that she had gone back to work when I started kindergarten because her doctor told her that she should. Or must. She needed to be something other than a mother and a wife. She needed to get out of the house. And that had pushed me out of the house, too, when I wasn't quite five and wasn't quite ready.

For a year after my botched beginnings at school and after I had routed my grandmother and Gus, I stayed home with "Huggy," Mrs. Huggins, a nanny of sorts. She was a relative by marriage to the lady next door, and my adoration of Ersal extended to her protégé. Huggy sat on the floor with me and taught me to read when I was still four. We chalked words on a board.

A is for Apple. B is for Boy. C is for Cat.

And for *Comfort*.

Huggy's big-boned body was fleshy and warm. Then she was gone. The explanation was odd. She broke her arm in a slamming car door while out for a drive with Ersal's jolly husband. Huggy did not have insurance and sued. By adult logic, that ended the friendship. I never saw Huggy again. I learned that relationships might sour very quickly. Love and its comforts could vanish as Huggy had. At least I could read, a life-long substitute for comfort.

The next year I tried school again.

In the first grade, I was determined to be a model of good behavior, but circumstances conspired against virtue. Evil was all around me. I was frightened and kept awake by a noise I heard each night. I told my teacher. Sister Mary Thomas explained to me in her brogue that it was the devil himself coming up the steps from the basement to get me because I was awake when I should be asleep. It was no comfort that I knew she was correct.

One Friday night, Daddy Jack gave me a penny for the two-for-a-cent gumball machine at the Kroger store. I chewed one tasteless gumball and thriftily tucked the second, a red one, into the pocket of my winter coat, under my mittens. The next Monday at school, as we walked the terrazzo halls on the way to recess, I pulled out my mittens but did not hear the renegade gumball hit the hard floor. I did not see it roll toward Sister Mary Thomas's tiny Irish feet. I was only thinking of the playground until all Catholic hell broke loose.

"Gumballs? Who brought gumballs to school? Who has the gumballs? Who?"

Begorrah!

I wanted to be good, and so I confessed. I was sent to the office of Sister Mary Blanche, the grim, slightly-hunched principal.

I now understood the genesis of sin.

It began with *gumballs*.

And gumballs came in pairs, two by two.

That same month, as I rode the lurching school bus, headed for another morning of sitting still at my desk and being a good first grader, the driver took a sharp right turn on to Richmond Road. I was tossed across the aisle and thrown against petite, pretty, and at all-points prissy Jo Rita Smith. Embarrassed, I covered the awkward physical contact by kissing her on the cheek.

Back I went to Sister Mary Blanche.

Apparently, "kissing girls" was a "near occasion of sin."

Kissing?

Worse than gumballs.

I thought of all the "sugar" demanded by aunts and all the huggy-kissy helloes and goodbyes from mother's lady-friends. And parental kisses, off-to-school kisses, and goodnight kisses. And there was Dinah Shore, throwing a kiss at a nation of Chevrolet drivers. "Mmmm-wah!" She seemed so *friendly*. So *pure*. I was confused.

But, I discovered, there was "kissing," and there was "*smooching*."

We had a babysitter who huddled for hours out in the driveway in the backseat of an old Dodge with her "cousin." They were *smooching*. We could see them through the steamy windows of the car when they came up for oxygen. We giggled and told Mother. Mother frowned and fired the teenager after only two passionate afternoons of kissing cousins at fifty cents an hour. Confusing.

My first school was a large Catholic institution in Lexington, and at recess, gumballs permitting, we were sent out onto a wasteland of blacktop to mill about with excessive supervision and minimal pleasure. A thick white line down the middle of the playground separated boys from girls, girls from boys. As we were in Kentucky, there were a few basketball goals on metal posts, on the *boys'* side. I tried to

play, but only once. I was the second smallest boy in the
class, but I tried. I stood expectantly under the net. I am
not sure what I imagined might happen, but a swishing ball
hit me hard on the head. It hurt, and a sensible voice in my
beleaguered skull announced, "That's it for sports. They're
not for you, Goose."

My nickname at home was "Goose." At first, my
brother and I called each other Goose. "Duck, Duck,
Goose." The name stuck to me. Later, I learned that the male
of the feathered species was a "gander." I was a Goose.

"Silly Goose!"

My baby-book records that at four my favorite
children's story was "Silly Hans." Silly Hans is the youngest
of three children, the one who can never do anything right.
He is a goose. A silly goose.

I never felt I looked like a "Kevin," anyway. My
name did not seem to fit my image of myself. Variations did
not help. I was never really a Kev, or worse, a Kevvie, except
sometimes to Aunt Chris and, later, to Joyce, my elderly English
actress friend. A cousin once called me "Kevvy-Chevy," which
I resented for its frivolity. For a time, I paid my brother a
quarter a week to call me "Bruin." I thought that being a
bear would make me a tough guy. We giggled in soprano
snorts. He took my money.

My sister loved Westerns, especially Roy Rogers and
his horse Trigger. She had a cowboy hat and a leather-fringed
skirt. To her cow-gal disgust, she received a "nun" doll for
Christmas. Despite her Barbie-revoking vows, the nun-doll had
a kewpie-mouth and lush eyelashes, but she was clad in black,
cinctured at the waist with a cloth rosary. Her veil was stapled
to her plastic head. It looked painful. And she was bald, like the
bloated monsignor. I peeked under the doll's veil to make this
discovery, but, of course, there was little reason to put hair on
a plastic nun whose headgear was so permanently fixed. I was
intrigued. One gusty day on the blacktop playground, just inside

the boy-side of the white line, I investigated. I watched as Sister Mary Theresa's veil lifted up and up and up behind her head in a winter wind. Moving in closer, I aided nature and lifted the black cloth higher. Was she like the doll? Bald?

All I ended up seeing was Sister Mary Blanche.

Back to the principal's office I went. Three strikes. Gumballs, Jo-Rita, and a hairless nun.

Silly Hans.

Duck, Duck, Silly Goose.

Something wasn't right. The world made that plain enough. I sensed somehow that it wasn't fair. I *knew*. It made me stubborn. And all the more desperate to be good.

The next year, my teacher was the same put-upon nun whose rosary I had savaged. The school had abolished its kindergarten, and from its ashes, Sister Rita Marie had risen to the second grade. She must have shuddered when she saw that I had come back to her, but she bragged that I was a "changed boy." I was *good*. The devil had apparently been properly exorcised, or, at least, it seemed so, for the moment.

I avoided the satanic monsignor whenever possible, but he cornered me to find out why my mother was not always at Sunday Mass. She was in danger of going to hell, he told me, because *he* had not seen her at Sunday Mass. I was nearly seven and speechless. I could not tell him of my mother's illnesses, the demons that I could not understand, let alone articulate.

We practiced for our First Communion. Sister Rita Marie showed us how to tent our hands upward in prayer. Allowing our hands to join in a downward-diving gesture, she warned us, indicated that we were choosing to pray to the devil. I was very, very careful to pray in the right direction, hands held in a tight steeple, above the *waist*. I had already heard Satan's footsteps on the basement stair and seen his fiery face in the kindergarten classroom. I desired no further knowledge of his Hell.

I remained a good boy in the third grade, where I encountered my first non-virgin schoolteacher. Mrs. Linacre was not a nun, but a "lay teacher." She was a married woman and rumored to be a Yankee. Later, when she got a divorce, the school banished her and would not speak her name. A divorced woman was a "fallen woman," unfit to be around impressionable young Catholics, who must grow up to marry once and forever and bring up their Catholic offspring to do the same, *in lux perpetua.*

By the third grade, I had a "girlfriend." I actually called her that. Ersal had moved to Florida. The Baxters now lived next door, and their eldest daughter was Ruth Helen. Two names. Very Southern. In the cramped suburbia of the late Fifties, Ruth Helen's bedroom window was no more than ten feet from mine. We would talk through the wire mesh screens, like going to Confession. On a squat spindle, I played 45s of the songs from *South Pacific.* I liked Mary Martin; I knew that she grew up to be Peter Pan who never grew up. I checked out the cast album of *Gypsy* at the library again and again. I sang along with Ethel Merman. Mary and Ethel. I sang show tunes to Ruth Helen Baxter. "Gonna Wash that Man Right Out of my Hair." "I'm in Love with a Wonderful Guy." "Everything's Coming Up Roses." "Let Me Entertain You."

"Sing out, Louise. Smile, Baby."

Ruth Helen grew up to be a lawyer. I grew up, sort of, to be an actor and a singer. When I was twenty-three, I belted out "There's No Business Like Show Business" at a benefit performance on a Broadway stage, standing next to Ethel Merman, also belting, albeit in a stronger light. Ms. Merman tongue-kissed me that night. That was later. Show business.

In 1960, Ruth Helen cried when I told her we were moving to the "country." She gave me her favorite hand puppet, a smiling tiger with soft paws and one glass eye. His other eye was an empty socket. I called him J. T. Tiger. To expand the casting potential for the short plays I devised for puppets, I borrowed a red dress from one of my sister's fashion dolls, pinned an old doll's eyelash over the space where J. T.'s missing tiger eye should have been, and presented him in an alternate persona. In a red dress, J. T. Tiger became "Je t-Aime Tiger." Tiger, puppet, one-eyed chanteuse. A feline Loretta Young, swirling into view with whiskers and a saucy wink.

A small drag queen on my right hand.

At least I did not strip the plastic nun and dress my puppet in her religious habit.

I wish I had.

My brother and I gave puppet shows, inflicting our shrill voices and nonsensical scripts on our long-suffering family and the trapped patients at a local nursing home. A decorative plastic-pearl top from a bottle of my mother's nail polish (*"Certainly Red"*) became an "ivory sword," the central plot device in one of our epics of giggled nonsense. At home, I housed my puppets in old cigar boxes in my bedroom closet. I could not assess my world coherently, but my imagination projected me for hours into the puppet universe. J. T. Tiger could be a dashing hero with a sword of ivory. Doubling and distressed in a red dress, he could be rescued.

In playing with puppets, I was, of course, playing with dolls.

Not a safe choice for a Kentucky boy.

With teary goodbyes to Ruth Helen, we moved to our five acres, just outside Versailles, fulfilling Grandfather Dearinger's unrealized dream of a place in the country. Daddy built us a "playhouse," a retreat for long afternoons of solitary reading: the Hardy Boys and Nancy Drew, books that could be read in a day. Old stacks of *Boy's Life* and *Mad Magazine*. Later, Daddy built us a treehouse, a reading platform swaying high in the green leaves, alarmingly close to the power lines. If you leaned on the tree trunk, you could hear an electric hum.

We still had a basketball hoop on a pole. My brother used it for a short time. I never did. It floated over my head, a flat orange zero.

Without air-conditioning, summers were long. The mind had time to drift. On humid nights, I could hear the insects screaming outside my bedroom. Sometimes, I would hear the clawing of some huge bug as it made its way up the window screen, trying to get in because it couldn't do so easily. The air was weighted with the smell of the mint from a nearby field.

Our little farm was an excellent training ground for solitude.

I now attended a small co-ed school, still Catholic, but in Versailles. Two rooms, four grades in each, one nun per room.

"Yes, Sister."

"No, Sister."

More blacktop at recess and lunch.

And I was a "good boy."

Goddammit!

Behind the school was a walnut grove, off-limits, and next door in an overgrown ravine was an abandoned train-tunnel, also off-limits. I was still afraid of demons in dark tunnels.

There were tall swings on the playground. Student legend insisted that an eighth-grade girl had once pumped her swing so high that she had gone over the top bar and come down on the other side, more or less intacta, "virgo" and otherwise. Or, said an alternate legend, she had broken both her legs and been permanently crippled. Punished for presumption and pride.

There was also a bell-shaped merry-go-round that

charted great metallic circles and waves around a central pole.
Another student legend: a fourth-grade boy had once been
squashed between the ring and the pole. The fourth-grade
boy's *middle* parts were smashed.

I was in the fourth grade.

With only twelve students in my class, I should have
made friends, but I didn't. Most of the boys had been held
back and made to repeat the third grade by a manifestly
vindictive nun, and so, as I was born late in the calendar
year, many of them were nearly two years older than I. By
the eighth grade, they practically shaved twice a day, while
I played with puppets and watched *Bewitched* and *The
Munsters*. I knew all the television theme songs and read *TV
Guide* in the grocery line to plan the two hours of television
I was allowed after homework and before nine-thirty.

The girls at school grew into giantesses. They were
competitive on the swing sets and vicious on the merry-
go-round. Shelia was funny. Jane was serene and beautiful;
when I read *Gone with the Wind*, I imagined her as Scarlett
to my hapless Charles Hamilton. Polly-Jean was bug-eyed
and shockingly blonde. With a mouth like a smug catfish,
Buddy-Ann had terrible posture and a perpetual scowl, and
if I felt sorry for her, which I did, she had no mercy for me.
Her commentary—on my appearance, my movement, my
speech, and my existence—was cutting, cruel, and relentless.
Bertha was whip-smart and stood with a wide stance, like a
well-worn cowboy, hot off the dusty trail. She preferred to
be called "Bertie." Lynn was wire-thin and quirky; she made
me laugh. Virgie was round-faced, tough and vulnerable, her
bangs cut square with a sensible slash.

Many of the girls had horses. They all *liked* horses.
It was Kentucky. There had been a girl back in Lexington
who whinnied, slapped her thigh, and galloped around
the neighborhood, but she was something of an equine
extremist.

I wanted them to like me, all of them, the boys and the girls. The horses.

For the most part, they didn't.

In the seventh and eighth grades, we walked to a grassy field after lunch and played softball in teams, divided not by a white line or even by gender, but on a judgment scale of physical maturity. Taut-armed Bertie and stocky-legged Virgie were skillful athletes, the first picked for teams, even before most of the boys. I tried with innocent fervor to join in the sport. I had not forgotten the feel of the basketball on my first-grade head, but I wanted to be liked. Wanting to be liked, however, did not guarantee aptitude. I was, perhaps deservedly, the last to be picked for a team, but the judgments I heard were not new to the world.

"You throw like a girl."

Buddy-Ann and Polly-Jean are grandmothers now; Bertie is a lawyer with a domestic "partner." Female. Virgie works for the homeless, a secular saint. Jane is still beautiful, still serene, tenderly creative, and in a brave manner, shy. We all grow up. We all grow older.

On the ball field, however, the girls all out-threw me, and I can only suppose that each of them "threw like a girl," too.

I practiced my softball skills at home, not quite alone. Throwing the ball in the air, I would smack it with a bat, and in the time that it was airborne, I would run the bases I had set up. Lady, our tireless border collie, would field the ball. If she got back to me with the ball before I rounded back to home-plate, she scored. If I outran her retrieval of the ball, I scored a point. Lady usually won. She left the ball wet with canine slobber, but this was the only sport I would ever enjoy playing and the only competition I would ever find comfortable. It helped that my only teammate and my only competition respected my efforts and I respected hers. We also shared a bed.

Back at school, Polly-Jean ran the bases with the

collie's speed and slightly less drool. She was my fifth-grade "girlfriend" for about a week, but when the engines of puberty revved up in every body but mine, I became the object of her advanced scorn. She flipped through my LP collection, pronouncing her verdict on each record album. "Cool," she would say from time to time in grudging approval, but usually she croaked, "Not cool. Not cool. Not cool." Coldly dismissive. Heartless with the onslaught of menses.

I could only hang my beardless chin in shame.

Looking back, however, I think, so *what* if I listened to Herman's Hermits and Petula Clark, and not the Rolling Stones? Peter Noone and Pet Clark sang in comfortable keys. I could sing along. And they sang of love, never sex. The Rolling Stones would put a zippered crotch on an album cover. Terrifying.

In my middle-school years, the "big boys," those strutting older boys in my class, the ones who lived on farms, raised cattle, rode horses, went to tractor-pulls, and said "pussy" when the nuns weren't listening, left me in a state of constant mortification. They despised me and jumped on every chance to reaffirm the rites and rights of the self-important alpha male. Ricky and Bobby were "pals," dressed like twins in rough jeans and tee-shirts when they could. I didn't like jeans. They were uncomfortable over my cotton boxers. Bobby and Ricky mocked the short pants I wore to a sixth-grade picnic. Apparently, real men in Kentucky, like proper Victorian ladies, did not show their legs. My scrawny legs were pale and hairless. I was sensitive enough to care that the other boys cared but defiant enough to keep on wearing my shorts.

I later learned that in Kentucky a "real man" also never carried an umbrella or wore a woolen scarf in the winter. *Real* men were expected to spit, swear, talk about "nice tits," arch hands-free at urinals, grunt dramatically on the toilet, not wash their hands, and break wind at either end without a "'scuse me."

Not all the local men were beasts of the Bluegrass jungle. Our family doctor was a young and handsome newlywed. He had a strong voice and a strong jaw, with a shadow beard of blue-black dots, like Superman. He drove a convertible, like a movie star. Unlike my first-cousin-once-removed, the reckless jay-bird, the doctor was fully clothed in his convertible. Men respected him. Women groaned. With teenage longing, my sister drooped at his sight and sighed, "There goes a hunk of man!" I knew he was more than five o'clock shadow and a sporty car. He was unashamed of being kind and being intelligent.

I also knew that I would never be considered "a hunk of man."

My father was also a good man and a *real* man, by any standards. I am grateful that he modeled a masculinity that did not insist on his sons being baboons. I felt guilty then, and still do, that I did not want to play basketball or toss a football, but my parents did not make athletics mandatory. I don't know what they thought of my softball games with the border collie, but they expected me to be kind. The Catholic Church expected me to be *good*. I tried to be both. Kind and good, or kinda good.

The Commonwealth of Kentucky preferred that I display the personality of a barn cat. I was supposed to be feral.

I went on wearing my shorts, sensible leg-wear in the Bluegrass humidity, but on other fronts, I was less defiant. Bobby and Ricky also mocked my smooth white hands, delicately feminine next to their chapped paws. *"Girl hands."* I went home and gouged the back of my hands with a sharp number-two pencil, stabbing and clawing the skin, hoping to destroy any trace of delicacy. Blue-black dots, self-inflicted.

Now, in my late sixties, I look down at my crinkled, spotted hands, hands that have held love and pushed it away. On some nights, I hate those unthinking boys more now than I did then. In the morning light, I am calmer.

I live with a few scars. Who doesn't?

Oh, yes, Ricky put mirrors on his shoes and tried to look up the dress of some semi-shocked, semi-titillated Catholic schoolgirl. Of *course,* he did. Not much happened as a result. Of course not. His behavior, I was made to understand, was considered *normal* boy behavior. Later, I would discover that mirrored shoes were part of urban legend. It was comforting to discover that on many levels Ricky was a cliché. But in his eyes, of course, so was I.

Our little parochial school had a policy for most kinds of behavior, and the rulebook positively prohibited "mixed parties," that is, parties attended by both boys and girls. To my surprise, Mother, usually in regimental lockstep with the Sisters of Divine Providence, fomented a small rebellion. She announced that *her* sons would certainly be allowed to attend and to host "mixed parties." I am sure she had her motives. I suspect she was nervous.

Polly-Jean, the queen of Cool and Not Cool, hosted several of these "mixed" parties. There weren't so many boys in the class that she could always avoid inviting me, and at her home, I first heard the Beatles and danced to "I Wanna Hold Your Hand." Oh, my poor scarred, scabby, white hands. Who would ever want to hold *them*?

I was also on an exclusive list of local Caucasian boys invited to attend the Saturday night dances at Margaret Hall, an Episcopal boarding and day school for young Caucasian ladies. The list was by way of a social stud service, and so I never knew how or why *I* was included. At my first "cotillion," the older revelers, high-school students, coupled in sweaty, slow-dance passion. The school gym was dark. The music yearned, and the dancers swayed, glassy-eyed with hormones. My assigned date and I sought refuge in the headmistress's office, chatting with that venerable old lady who spoke with an English accent because she was Episcopalian, not because she was English, which she wasn't. She showed us her collection of miniature dinosaurs. While my young-for-her-age date and I played with plastic sauropods, the more mature couples groped each other to the rhythms of the Righteous Brothers, in search of "that lovin' feeling." I had no idea what that feeling might be. I thought it might be better than loneliness but reasoned that it was probably another sin, not quite righteous, and by all appearances, rather sweaty. My innocence was not willful, but it might just as well have been. Margaret Hall dropped me off the "cotillion" list after two dances.

Not Cool.

Margaret Hall girls had a rumor-driven reputation for being wild. We all supposed that the boarding students had been sent away from home because their libidos required some sort of velvet-barred puberty-prison. There were tales of dining hall food laced with saltpeter. These young women sometimes dated local boys, all on the sly. Several, it was whispered, were "having sex" with young gentleman of color. Local prejudice mandated that they meet in odd but private spaces. When I later worked at the public library, the only male employee, I was sent to knock on the ladies' room door and shoo out the copulating couples. By then, I was a very virginal sixteen.

(Knock, knock, knock.)

"Uh, 'scuse me, but could you come out of there. Please?"

(Knock, knock, knock.)

"Sorry to bother you, but the librarian lady says you need to come out of the restroom."

(Knock, knock, knock.)

"Please."

They called me "Icky-bod Crane."

Bad Sex in Kentucky

One of the boarding-school girls stole my jacket, the only article of clothing I owned that came within striking distance of "cool." It was a belted "bush jacket." Probably "not cool" after all, but then why steal it?

Margaret Hall closed a few years later. More whispers. By day, the girls played field hockey, but at night, said the rumors, the school harbored a "ring of lesbians." Why, I wondered, did lesbians come harbored and in rings? Like pirate ships, international spies, and the circles of Saturn.

Oh, to be a sexual outlaw in a small Kentucky town. I only wish I had been.

I wasn't even sure what a lesbian was. Or did.

Back in elementary school, however, my brother and I were allowed to host our own "mixed parties." Mother and Daddy hovered nearby. Chips were em-bowled, and squat bottles of Coca-Cola stood ready amid chunks of clear ice. My brother decreed that no party was complete without a silver bowl of cashews. He was being amusing in his self-aware fashion, and I laughed, but I also took him seriously, ever the younger brother, looking for guidance. Salted cashews were duly enshrined in a silver (plated) bowl on a side table.

We partied. The stacks of LPs and 45s were spindle-spitted and scratched into revelation by the phonograph needle. *Cool. Not Cool.*

I was small and agile and easily won the limbo competitions, solo. A one-man game of Twister. *Not Cool.*

Slow dances with a partner proved more perplexing. Where to put your hands, how close to hold your partner, and how long to look directly into your partner's face? A bit, I found out somewhat later, like the sex act itself.

Clever boy!

The fast dances were often too intricate to be learned by observation, and I had no one to teach me.

Here I abandon the sex-act simile.

Or perhaps, sadly, I don't.

I invented a dance of my own that seemed to amuse everyone, or at least my brother, always my most important audience. I would release my backbone and gyrate like a wayward hydra in a swirl of sea currents. I called it "The Spineless." I should have called it "The Sexless." It was another solo performance. Vaudeville.

"Oh, that crazy Kevin!"

Back when she would still speak to me and we exchanged school pictures, Polly-Jean once wrote on the back of her photo, "To Kevin, the kookiest kid in the seventh grade." Full marks, Polly-Jean, for combining creative spelling and alliteration with satiric euphemism!

My brother was better at the whole social game and proudly "danced every dance," with his moderate Beatle-bangs sticking wetly to his forehead. When he was truly in the mixed party spirit, he would grab Bertie and Polly-Jean as his backup singers and entertain the crowd with a lip-synched rendition of "You Keep Me Hanging On." As an encore: "Stop in the Name of Love," with appropriate hand gestures. He was a marvelous Diana Ross.

I had my own party-time personality. More than once I pretended to dance the tango. In public. Exotic. Alone. And, yes, with a rose in my teeth. I had seen it in a movie. All I needed was a bowl of bananas on my head.

And yet, from time to time, beautiful Jane would consent to share a slow dance with me. I worried that I was somehow letting her down, but her soft cheek and soft shoulders, touched lightly with a modest perfume, were a haven of safety and acceptance. I was grateful but too terrified to tell myself why. I hoped she would understand.

Bertha, Polly-Jean, Buddy-Ann, Virgie, Ricky, Bobby, and the others came to our "mixed parties" and ate our cashews from the silver-plated dish, but behind our backs and still within earshot, they called us "the Dearinger girls." My brother tells me that the phrase was "the Dearinger sisters." Either way, there was no effective response. Protest the comment? Try to disprove it? Ignore it? Joke about it? We could only pray that our parents did not hear the slur.

Some compass was spinning, but the course had been settled long ago. Surely, sexual identity may be discovered, but not charted.

The treachery occurs when others discover your identity before you do.

And try to make it something it is not.

Dirty. Shameful. Wrong.

Somehow, however, we continued to trust that all would be well. My brother bent his head over the piano keys and played hymns and old ballads from the *Golden Book of Songs*. He would pound out show tunes, and I would belt out the lyrics, aiming in my mind at some top balcony, hoping, somehow, for applause. Or approval. I sang show tunes to clear my mind of reality.

At night I prayed myself to sleep with the rosary in my hand.

At a late August picnic, a mosquito bit the side of my neck, just at the collar line. Being the "nervous type," I scratched the itchy bump. The initial bite flared into an angry red sore. When classes started for my eighth-grade year, I wore the welt without thought, at least until Ricky made a new issue of it. "Hickey," he shouted, pointing at my red blotch. "Hickey! Hickey! Hickey! Passion Mark! Passion Mark!" A hormonal crowd gathered to gawk. For a moment I imagined that I might transform this latest embarrassment into triumph. They all seemed fascinated. And deeply repulsed. Unfortunately, I had no idea what a "hickey" or a "passion mark" could possibly be. I had only heard of the "Passion of

Christ." I understood the stigmata and was quickly learning the notion of stigma. I prayed every night, with that rosary in my scratched and virginal hands, that I would be a saint. I was willing to try.

About this time, I read *Dracula* for the first time. I was unaccountably breathless when Stoker's protagonist waited in "languorous ecstasy" as the vampire's three brides crept upon supine Jonathan Harker for a feeding and the blonde one licked her lips and breathed hotly on his bared neck. (Not unlike our border collie hovering over sleepy Aunt Christine). I read this passage aloud several times to myself without grasping the fact that I was luxuriating in late-Victorian soft pornography.

I acted it out.

I surprised my seventeen-year-old sister with the announcement that I was "a vampire" and had come to "drink her blood." I then bit her neck, not hard, but with enough fang to leave my mark. I did not understand her furious embarrassment. I did not understand that a high school girl was not likely to enjoy explaining to her classmates that the purple bruise on her neck had been put there by her brother.

This was going too far. Even in Kentucky,

And so, when my irritated mosquito bite excited the libidinous imaginations of my Catholic classmates, I was just confused. Clueless. And then the nun, Sister Alma Joseph, all chins and horror, stepped in and demanded to know what all the fuss was about. All I could think of was "Gumballs!" She dragged me in shame to the front of the classroom and pulled down the collar of my shirt with astonishing ruthlessness. My red wound burned like the mark of Cain.

"Is *this*," she shrieked, pointing at my neck, "is *this* the outcome of *mixed parties*?"

More confusion.

I liked women. I was not attracted to them, but I *liked* them.

I was not sure I liked men. They certainly did not like me.

I did not like me much either. I wasn't allowed to.

I tried to understand the world of boy-girl, boy-girl, boy-girl.

We had some sex education.

Some.

Mother was tight-lipped on the topic. My sister has no memory of "the talk," but I heard all the mumbling among the womenfolk when my sister "became a *woman*." What, I wondered, had she been in all the years previous to this transformation? A cow-gal? There was a blue box in the cabinet under the bathroom sink; my brother and I were told not ever to touch it. Women were a mystery.

So were men.

But "sex" had *something* to do with women, with Marilyn Monroe and Jayne Mansfield, large breasts, tight clothes, blonde hair, and premature death.

I had been born the day after Thanksgiving. Mother had eaten a holiday dinner with her family and then gone to the hospital for a Caesarean section, all pre-planned and arranged. Aunt Chris was not told; she got "nervous." Something *bad* might have happened to her sister. For most of my early life, I thought that babies came when a mommy ate too much turkey.

Thanksgiving indigestion still makes me nervous.

When I was twelve, Daddy gave his sons a book to explain "sex." Perhaps my brother's sketched-in moustache signaled that the time had come, and I was economically included in the required reading, but it was far too soon.

I was a clever reader, but I could make little of the mysterious veils that *Into Manhood, a Guide for Boys* promised and failed to lift. There was a diagram in floppy profile of the male genitalia, with arrows and lines pointing out the testes, the scrotum, the prostate, and something called the "vas deferens." I read about "nocturnal emissions" and "painful breast knots" with wondering stupidity. I tried to understand why I was supposed to know something new about my "doogee," as my brother and I still called the penis, when we spoke of it at all, which despite sharing a bedroom and a few early baths, we rarely did.

The shared baths ended when I was eight. After that it was "too icky," and I never again saw my brother naked. We moved our beds as far apart as our shared room would allow. When we changed in a locker room to go swimming, we avoided eye contact, retreated to dark corners, and never looked around. More often, we wore our bathing suits to the pool under our summer shorts and came home without removing the wet bathing gear, just shuffling into our shorts again, leaving wet imprints of our backsides, never our "butts," on the car seats. Mother called our fastidious modesty "foolishness."

Into Manhood offered neither guidance nor comfort. The droopy spigot in the penile diagram was as fat and foreign as the limp noodles at Wing's Tea House. The book might as well have been written in Mandarin. It offered no comparable diagram of the female anatomy. The book's queasy authors must have worried that such an illustration might prove too alluring to the pre-teen boy.

The *normal* boy.

The book warned against the evils of masturbation. I thought the *word* sounded interesting. I liked long words, but the act itself remained unfathomable. Attempting such a deed in close proximity to my rosary beads might mean self-mutilation, and *Into Manhood* was not authorized to serve as a "how-to" manual to this dark mystery. Was I supposed to know how to do this on my own? Was I *broken* down there? The book hinted, darkly indeed, that the habit of self-pleasure might later interfere with the happiness of marriage and parenting. It might, however, have tempered the deluge of "nocturnal emissions" and, who knows, even reduced the agony of "painful breast knots."

On the subject of homosexuality, *Into Manhood*

was even grimmer. It warned of "some sick men," who might lure a young boy into something dangerous, deadly, and evil. With what was probably intended as enlightened understanding in 1964, the book coldly explained that these "homosexuals" were lonely men who would never know the felicity of fatherhood. Their "sickness" was to be pitied—and reported posthaste to parents and police, as well as, of course, to trustworthy scoutmasters, ministers, and priests.

None of this seemed to have anything to do with me.

Daddy may have been sexually molested when he was eleven or twelve. He accepted a ride in a car with a stranger. The stranger "tried something." *Something?* No details on that front. Daddy escaped unharmed, or at least I hope that the story ended that way. He never told us this cautionary tale, but he told Mother at some point, and she repeated the story to us with some regularity. She wanted, I am sure, to scare us into safety. She certainly made us uncomfortable.

Sick?

Lonely?

More to be pitied?

Strangers in cars.

We were given a second sex manual, an understudy pamphlet with an unpromising super-specialist title: "What Every Eighth Grade Catholic Boy Should Know about Sex."

It was a remarkably *short* volume.

Its pithy paragraphs proclaimed that women were the "Temples of God" and that chastity was the legacy of the Blessed Virgin Mary, the BVM. We had long heard of Maria Goretti and Dominic Savio, pretty Italian saints who chose mutilation and martyrdom rather than the rendering up of their virginity. Being a Catholic publication, "What Every Eighth Grade Catholic Boy Should Know about Sex" said less on the subject of masturbation than *Into Manhood,* but in a particularly risible chapter, it gingerly stroked that super-sensitive topic. The text struggled earnestly to detail the manner by which a rampantly errant Catholic boy might confess to a priest in the dark privacy of the confessional that he had committed a sin of "impurity." The priest might then ask, "alone or with others."

Others?

I trembled.

The pamphlet also sternly warned against euphemisms, dishonest imprecisions of language employed to mask the sin of "self-abuse." Under no circumstances were such sins to be detailed to the breathless confessor in crude street terms. Telling "the good father" that you had "jerked off" or "rubbed one out" was not acceptable. Nor was a sinful boy permitted to cloak his iniquity by describing his genital transgression as "making the Blessed Virgin cry."

Making the Blessed Virgin cry?

What would Dominic Savio have done? "Death rather than sin," he had resolved, blissfully prepubescent at the age of seven.

I am horrified now to realize that at eleven, twelve, or thirteen, not seven, I would have made the same choice as young Dominic, but at eleven, twelve, and thirteen, not seven, I did not understand any of this, except that much of it seemed a bit silly. I still played with puppets. Busy hands…and so on.

And, oh, I had an ant farm, another of Kevin's imitations of life.

There was a third "sex" book, of sorts. If my parents ever told sexually suggestive jokes when I was growing up, I never heard them, but at some point, a book of bawdy jokes mysteriously appeared in our house. It was a gift book, one that my parents were too polite to discard, but instead of joining the long rows of respectable books on the den wall, this book, *Furthermore Over Sexteen*, lived its dank life on a low shelf in the linen closet. Not exactly *between* the sheets, but *under* them. The red-jacketed volume contained a series of racy cartoons and anecdotes, often involving leering men cavorting with large-breasted women in diaphanous nighties. It was all very suggestive, but suggestive of *what*, I had no idea. The book eventually disappeared. When I was somewhere in my mid-twenties, I woke up in the middle of the night, blushing with a delayed understanding of some of the punch lines.

Ah-ha! (*Ha-ha.*)

Reading those jokes before and during puberty, I felt excluded. Remembering them as an adult, I still feel excluded.

From time to time, Mother referred to childbirth as "the pain that only a woman can know." Back in the sixth grade, I discovered "the pain that only a *man* can know" and that only a supremely careless boy can induce. Mother had frugally recycled our outgrown trousers, snipping off the cuffs, adding rope belts, and presenting us with "beach-combers" for the summer months. *This* in Kentucky, a state that already had little use for boys who wore shorts. I did not really mind. I did not really care. The pants, however, were tight and merciless on expanding bodies. They body-hugged like Capri pants on a Hollywood starlet.

I had remained shy in locker rooms and public bathrooms. In a men's room near my father's office at the University of Kentucky, I rushed to get away from a urinal before a stranger came in, and I snagged my foreskin in the zipper of my too-tight beach-combers. I tried to disengage. No luck. I held a paper bag in front of my pants and sought out my father in his office. He advised me. Nothing budged. He took me to my pediatrician. I told Dr. Wheeler that I had hurt my "doogee." Calmly, Daddy suggested it was time I called it a "penis," and so I did. "Oh," crooned Dr. Wheeler with cheerful nonchalance, "one good yank will do the trick." And with that, he gave my penis his

89

one good yank. Jesus help me! Was *this* masturbation? As
the doctor yanked his yank, my foreskin let function follow
form. It stretched. It stretched and stretched and stretched,
like a bungee cord, and although the flesh shredded like an
old bedsheet, my youthful doogee held on. The pain was
white. I saw nothing but a blinding light and do not know
if I screamed. I know I would now. Then, I only knew that
zippers were built to last and that this would be my final visit
to Dr. Wheeler. In every life there comes a time to move on
from a pediatrician.

Now, less calm, Daddy rushed me to a hospital
emergency room, and I saw another white light, the light
of the operating room. White-masked faces hovered over
me, as, full of white painkillers, I floated away into whiteness.
Daddy stayed nearby. I remember being home again, sore, and
then sorer, and then back to the hospital with an infection. An
infection "down there." My parents never left my side. When
I returned home, Polly-Jean and Shelia, my makeshift
"girlfriends" of the time, called to see what was wrong. This
was not something I could tell them. I heard my mother on
the phone, telling Aunt Chris my sad and humiliating story.
She whispered the words, but I heard every intimate vowel
and stinging consonant.

In middle-age, I discovered that my brother had
shared this story with many of his friends. They looked at
me oddly, and I laughed. They would have laughed, too, if
they had seen what remained "down there." To free me from
my zipper's teeth, the surgeon had performed what he called a
"dorsal slit." I am, for all intents and purposes, *half*-circumcised,
cowled like a Trappist monk, hanging from his heels in the apse.

The learning curve is what it is.

Speaking of dicks—and the history of my dorsal slit
invariably moves me to gleeful crudity—a few words about
Ricky, the bully, to finish him off. He tormented me beyond
elementary school. When I was a high school junior, he

spotted me walking down Main Street in Versailles. He was in his pick-up truck, probably with a gun rack in the rear window. Probably with a dead animal in the truck bed. Possibly with a butchered pet buried in his back yard. Or worse. I had not seen him in several years. He slowed the truck, rolled down a window, and yelled, "Fag!"

Actually, he screeched.

"Faaaaaaaaaaaaaaaaaag!"

I pretended that I had not heard him. I had.

He possessed the lungs of a practiced hog-hollerer.

I did not see Ricky again for nearly forty years. I was at a Christmas home-show in Lexington with my sister and her daughter. My sister pointed out an older man who stood across the convention hall, with his stooped back to us, his neck red above his shirt collar. He had a bald patch on the back of his head. I could not see his face. "Do you know who that is?" asked my sister. I did not. "Well, that's Ricky, the guy from your eighth-grade class," she told me.

My first impulse was to go over and re-introduce myself. I had learned that many school bullies later regret their cruelties and grow up to be decent human beings. Eventually.

Then I stopped myself. What, I thought, if he were unchanged? What if now, after all this time, he sneered again and called me a "fag?"

"Faaaaaaaaaaaaaaaag!"

Surrounded by cheery holiday decorations, I wondered if I might then batter him to death with an artificial Christmas tree or impale him on a plastic reindeer, life-sized for the lawn and illumined from within?

I did not go over. I did not speak and did not introduce myself. I turned away.

By spring of the next year, he was dead, a heart attack.

My brother asked if I planned a celebration; perhaps I might throw a "mixed party," he joked. No, I virtuously replied, proud for a moment of what I thought must be my moral superiority. People change. I had grown up. I was an adult, not a vulnerable boy. And Ricky was, or had been, a father and a grandfather, a hard-working farmer, struggling in a dying industry. He surely had grown, transformed. Matured. Death, even the death of a long-ago bully, was nothing to celebrate.

So I told my brother.

A few months later, on a sweltering July afternoon, I stopped at a cemetery to visit the graves of my maternal grandparents. Albert and Ada lie side by side in one of those soulless boneyards, austerely Protestant, that mandates flat markers to make mowing the turf easier. No fresh flowers, please, but row on row of identical urns holding faded artificial blossoms. Bits of plastic stems and nearly colorless cloth litter the ground, chewy bits for the cemetery mowers on a rolling plain of desolation and grief, with no comfort but the wide sky.

Even the glaring sky offered little comfort that day. If the eye of heaven watched over that July afternoon, it watched in Baptist wrath. White and relentless.

I remembered that a great-uncle, another of the silent brood, had recently been buried nearby. I struck off, up a hill, looking for the old man's grave. Before I found Uncle Truman, however, I came upon a flat stone with the image of a tractor on it. Very Kentucky. Curious, I looked at the name on the stone. Ricky. It was Ricky.

I was standing on his grave.

I paused.

Out of nowhere, an Italian folk tune ran through my head, that jaunty Neapolitan tarantella, the one that underscores stereotypical scenes of "happy Italian peasants," cavorting in their dusty village streets. "Dum-di-dum-di-dum-di-dum-di-dum-di-dum-ditty-dum."

I lifted a foot.

I skipped.

No, I danced.

I danced on Ricky's grave.

After a long delay, crudity had answered cruelty.

I think that this is the worst thing I have ever done in my life.

At least I did not urinate.

Back in elementary school, I did eventually find two friends. Timmy and Chuck were a year behind me at the Catholic school in Versailles, but they were closer to me in age than most of the boys in my class.

We were a clumsy trio. We bonded over our shared immaturity. The qualities that we had in common were innocence, denial, and an appreciation of the absurdity of popular culture. We spoke on the phone at length every night. We giggled rather than laughed. Chuck's father said I was "too silly for a boy," but I was happy to have friends. They seemed to like me. They seemed *like* me. We pledged loyalty.

And then I had to go to high school.

Kevin Lane Dearinger

Chapter Eight

High School, Alone and with Others, Mostly

Catholics

Most of my eighth-grade classmates cheerfully abandoned Catholic education as they swan-dived into high school. They took their places with the country kids at the county school. Each in our time, however, my siblings and I were sent to the region's Catholic high school, a low-slung dullness of pale-orange brick, with utilitarian classrooms and narrow, terrazzo-paved halls, among other cold comforts. Catholic education seemed to prize the uncompromising practicality of terrazzo. More vulnerable, the ceilings of insulated tiles were pocked with the lumps of paper wads, masticated and fired when some nun or doddering priest was not looking. Practice shots in preparation for a more elemental battle. Rehearsal ejaculation.

The Catholic school was ripe with sex.

Sex seemed to drive every look, every shove in the hall, every punch in the lunch line, and every profanity that roared from my classmates. Ricky had gone to the county school to join the Future Farmers, but the Catholic high school kenneled his clones. Some pushed me into walls. Others just walked by, not sure what to make of me. I tried to make friends. I tried to make truces. We were all struggling to figure out who and what we were. For some, self-definition was a matter of marginalizing others,

95

constructing inclusion by ruthless exclusion.

There was a boy named Daniel Boone. "Now," I thought, "this is *so* Kentucky!" I was going to school with "Dan'l Boone." Sensing the absurd had become my best protective measure.

Daddy Jack drove us to school on his way to the university. To celebrate our five-acre "baby farm," he had purchased a dark green 1951 Chevy pickup truck. It might have belonged to the Beverly Hillbillies. My discreet brother had Daddy drop him off around the corner from the school, but I was happy to let him drive me right up to the door outside my homeroom. Every morning, I kissed him goodbye on the cheek. As I came in the school door, I would hear kissy-sounds and, "Hey, Sweetie."

Or sometimes just, "Queer." At times, that terrifying word emerged in several syllables. "Qeeee-errr." Usually, it came out in a stunted Kentucky monosyllable: "Quaar."

My school picture from freshman year preserves evidence of my defenseless adolescence. My skin is clear and almost paper-white, with a few freckles across my thimble of a nose. My hair is ragged. My ears are flappy. My sweater is cardigan. My eyes are trusting. My smile is childlike or childish, and I recognize even now my old look of aspiring sainthood. I soon learned to shield my sense of self in school pictures with a serious or seriously blank expression on my face.

I was tiny. Scrawny. On the first day of P. E., under the coach's orders, I tried to hoist my head above a bar in a "chin-up," but the best I could manage was to hang there like a dead rabbit. I dangled for a long time. The coach finally told me to let go. He was openly disgusted.

He ordered us all to the showers.

Determined to do something right that day, I obeyed.

I struggled against my old fear of public nakedness. I chucked off my shoes and white socks, my tee-shirt (Boy's

Small), my gym shorts (Boy's Small), and my athletic supporter (Junior). I had one of my sister's old beach towels, decorated with anchors and life-preservers. I wrapped it around my hairless loins.

Printed on the towel in friendly salutation: "Ahoy there, sailor!"

I padded into the inner locker room, a windowless, pitiless vault. I did not know that I had invaded the exclusive domain of the most powerful jocks, forbidden territory for the unmanly prepubescent. I did hope that if I hurried, I could be wet, dried-off, and gone before anyone else arrived. I dropped my towel and stepped into the utilitarian-tiled, no-stalls, all-together-in-the-altogether showers. I stood in the stone-cold crotch of the terrazzo-souled school.

At first, I looked at nothing. With glazed eyes, I tried thinking of Dominic Savio and Maria Goretti, those Italian virgins I still hoped to join. I managed to soap up and had begun to rinse off when several other boys stepped into the steamy water. Above our heads, white light bulbs glared from tight metal traps.

We were all high-school freshmen. In class, we wore similar shirts and ties and trousers, but in the shower, we had little in common. The others had their own nervousness, covered with profanity, flicking towels, and furtive, defiant glances. To prevent eye contact, for I truly feared that they might kill me, I looked *down.*

"Down" was a big mistake.

While puberty had not had much to say to my boy-body, a more advanced hormonal surge had pushed these *boys* into manifest manhood. Chad, who was not as friendly as his sitcom name, had a forest of dark chest hair and legs like a satyr, with equipment in between that could by no measure be dismissed as a "doogee." He looked older than my pediatrician. He soaped and flopped and rinsed and flopped. He always had an Elvis sneer on his face, but I wasn't looking at his face.

I was horrified.

There was still more to see that I did not want to see.

I turned in the shower and saw Daniel Boone. Dan'l of Old Kaintuck. The historical Boone was then a character on a television show. "Daniel Boone was a man, yes, a *real* man," according to the opening theme song. This Daniel Boone, a high-school freshman, had the body of a "real man," a middle-aged, beer-drinking, pool-shooting, trucker-cap-wearing, Peterbilt-driving man. A belly under a pelt of wild-animal fur, and then a weary tube that looped out of matted curls like a melting can of Campbell's Tomato Soup. Dali and Warhol in a Catholic locker room. Such metaphors, of course, came later. At the time, I had nothing to which I might compare these sights. I had never before seen a naked man, let alone, naked *men*. Either I was showering with aliens or they were showering with a freak.

I fled that room of revelations and never returned. None of this was erotic. It was accidental education. Directed by Roger Corman.

The only men's room in the school, condescendingly marked "Boys," offered another nightmare. It was the popular smoking den for those who underscored their masculinity by destroying their lungs. The room reeked of smoke and urine and worse. The priests had removed the doors to the cubicles. There would be no privacy if you needed it. No hurried self-abuse was going to take place in this hallowed hellhole. The urinal was a foul trough, a too-much-shared experience if you ducked in to relieve yourself between classes. Trying to pee meant a watery dueling match in an elongated sink. I remember going into that foul cavern no more than a handful of times in four years. I am sure I squirmed in discomfort in math and history and skimped on lunch to better my odds of making it home before nature called.

This was not delicacy. This was survival.

The classrooms offered no refuge. Most of the desktops were booby-trapped with gum underneath and profanity above. The words carved and inked on the desktops were mostly new to me. I had been sheltered more than most. My parents never swore or used "bad language" in front of us. The "butt" in Mother's nervous tirade had shocked me when I was four. Someone, probably the Yankee boy one street over, had painted "Fuck" on a lamp-post near our house in 1959. The word stayed there for some time, menacing even as it faded, but never mentioned.

When we were children, Mother never acknowledged the infamous "F-Word," and years later, when she did at last mention her offense at a carelessly dropped "F-Word," it soon became clear that she meant "fart." She would not have liked Chaucer. Mother did mention the "S-Word," as in, "Boys, your cousin used the S-Word at your grandmother's house today. I hope you boys will never use that kind of language." On a trip to California, however, before she married Daddy, she had pondered the Hollywood gossip she somehow heard. Cary Grant and Randolph Scott were "queer," she wrote in a letter home. Paulette Goddard, too, "probably."

And so, I was very protected, more or less, but in high school, it suddenly seemed that language, words and phrases not familiar to the Hardy Boys, could be sinful.

Sexual, and, therefore, sinful.

Sometimes the words were made flesh in drawings, usually the depiction of sketchy genitals surrounded by inky hair. One drawing, a penis that grew into a mountaintop and became a volcano in vehement eruption, stuck in my mind with uncomfortable clarity.

The words were exotic: pussy, dick, cock, eat me, suck it, and in one audacious statement by some daring boy wielding a wicked ballpoint Bic, *cunt*.

I did what I thought was sensible. I made a list of the offending mysteries, went to the library, and looked up each word in the unabridged dictionary. Some were there. Some were not. So much for unabridged. The dictionary was circumcised. A dorsal slit of censorship.

Conversations overheard before homeroom or when the teacher left the classroom were alarming. One hammer-headed boy, who lived in a rough neighborhood downtown, announced that his father, presumably an adult, had told him that women had "teeth down *thar*." And if you put your "wang in *thar*," it would be bitten off and swallowed. This was information left unexplored by *Into Manhood*. It sounded like a good subplot on *The Munsters* but not probable. I did not quite know what to think. Only in graduate school would I hear again of the "vagina dentata." From where, I still wonder, in the screwy masculine psyches of our culture could such a misogynistic notion spring?

If only I had asked Aunt Chris.

I had no personal fear, however, that my "doogee" might become a vaginal snack. Girls now ignored me. There were exceptions, but the general rule that emerged from experience was that the larger breasts a girl had, the less likely it was that she would speak to me. Barbara, exceedingly flat-chested Barbara, was nice to me. She spoke in an endearing squeak, and the boys called her The Mouse. I liked The Mouse. With her sweet face and a kerchief tying back her hair, she did look as if she might sew up a nifty dress for Disney's "Cinder-relly."

High school social logic reduced Barbara to "a mouse." I was not yet judged to be a man.

The rules and standards were unwritten but rigorously enforced. No one carried a book bag, and there were no backpacks. Schoolbooks were to be stacked on a three-ring binder. A boy was expected to balance the assembled items under one arm, with the bulk resting on his hip. Only a girl would carry her books clutched in the front of her body, high or low. Only a girl needed to cover and defend that area.

There were exceptions to this hard rule, exceptions well known to every boy and noted by more than a few blushing girls. The school demanded that boys wear their shirttails tucked in at the waist, but when a wandering mind and a hormonal tsunami produced a sudden frontal prod, the shirts were untucked and, in extreme cases, binders and books rotated front as a sturdy fig leaf. What the teachers thought, I can only imagine. The nuns had vowed chastity but not stupidity. What some of the priests thought still makes the Vatican shudder.

Other tests of manliness were more insidious.

"Quick, look at your fingernails!"

If you held out your hand, palm down, fingers curved for inspection, you were "a girl" or "a queer" or, with high-school logic, "both." A *real* boy would scrunch his fingers into a claw-like fist. Rough.

"You have something on your shoe!"

If you lifted the foot behind you, your masculinity was suspect. *Real* boys would twist a foot up in front of the other leg, like the old statue of the naked boy removing a thorn from his foot.

At some point in my freshman year, someone circulated a "Virginity Test." It came in the form of a series of questions that escalated in erotic inquisition.

Have you kissed a girl?

Have you kissed a girl on the mouth?

Have you kissed a girl on the mouth while wearing pajamas?

Have you kissed a girl on the mouth while wearing pajamas in a bed?

Have you kissed a girl on the mouth in a bed without pajamas?

And so on.

(And under what circumstances, Groucho, does a bed wear pajamas?)

The boys in my homeroom thought I would be a fitting stooge for this test, but I astonished them by answering "yes" to

most of the questions. I was a good test-taker and had quickly
figured out the tricks and turns of this particular quiz. I had, of
course, kissed my *mother* goodnight as I toddled off to bed in
my Sleepy Boy flannel pajamas. I thought I was clever, but I am
sure the boys knew I was a liar. With such Jesuitical equivocation,
I *was* a liar, but I wonder what lies the others told? And I wonder
what boy-virgin first concocted that Virginity Test?

It sure as hell wasn't Dominic Savio.

As a freshman, I stood five-two and weighed one-
hundred-twenty-five pounds. By mid-year as a sophomore,
I was five-eleven, and still one-hundred-twenty-five-pounds.
My nose added horizontal inches to the stretch. I had no
idea how much and *where* I had grown until Red Davy asked
me one day before school if he could copy my homework
answers. My prim morality would only permit me to offer to
show him how he might find the answers for himself, and I
took on a professorial tone as I explained how he, too, might,
with steady effort, virtuously complete his own homework.
"Damn," I heard Red Davy whisper to one of his cronies,
"look, at his nose. It's *huge*."

As a high school freshman, I had still not made the
"Blessed Virgin" cry, but nature can be insistent. "Nocturnal
emission" sounded like what your auto engine might do on
its own, overnight in the garage, and in a way, that is what
it was. *Into Manhood* had put the term in my head, but
the reality was as confusing as the dreams I had and only
half-remembered. Mother changed my bedsheets without
comment.

At some point, late in puberty, I joined the human
race and masturbated. In my journal, I swore that with the
help of JesusMarynJoseph I would never, never, never do *that*
again. I did not feel sinful, however, only lonely and a bit
unclean.

Broken.

I thought I had "leaked."

I went to confession and mumbled something about a "sin of impurity" through the screen to the leaning head of the listening priest. "Alone or with others?" he asked.

JesusMarynJoseph!

Of course, I was ALONE!

Biology class was biologically useless. The humorless coach un-taught the course. He would assign chapters to read in the text and give mimeographed, multiple-choice tests from the teacher's edition. He was rarely even in the biology lab. One day, he assigned groups, allotted each group a dead frog, told us to follow the diagram for dissection in our books, and went back to his office near the gym to chain smoke. My mother had fainted when dissecting a rabbit in a college course and so ended her dreams of becoming a doctor. (Doctor, not nurse! Good for you anyway, Mother!) I was determined to be braver. Without adult supervision, however, chaos ruled the high-school lab. Predictably, frog parts were severed without scientific care. Also predictably, the usual villains pelted me with frog legs, frog heads, and frog guts.

This absentee-teacher was the same coach who had ordered me to the horrors of communal showering in my freshman year. Reeking of cigarette smoke, he was also my instructor in Health, another read-the-book, fill-in-the-worksheets class. On his first fill-in-the-blank (easy-to-grade between cigarettes) test, we were asked to "name three venereal diseases." The sum of my knowledge came from a short, ambiguously-worded paragraph in my dog-eared paperback textbook, about which we not been allowed to ask questions. I looked at the three blanks on the test paper. Carefully, and with correct spelling, I wrote "syphilis" and "gonorrhea." The former was a particular spelling challenge in Kentucky, where it was pronounced, in a whisper, as "gon-ah-rear." So, "syphilis" and "gonorrhea." And? *And?* Only decades later would the world have the

terrible initials HIV and AIDS to fill that third blank so
devastatingly. In 1965, I could not think of a third sexually-
transmitted disease. If sex remained a mystery, its diseases
were inexplicable. I was too good a test-taker to leave a blank
answer, and at the end of the period, I quickly penciled in
the only other slightly disgusting ailment that our prudish
textbook had broached. Summer Diarrhea. "Di-ah-rear." This
apparently caused some hilarity in the coach's smoky office,
especially on the test of a "good boy" and A-student. He
called in my parents and cautioned them that they would
need to take greater care in parenting me. A thirteen-year-
old son who could not identify three venereal diseases was
surely a disgrace to family, to education, and to manhood.
I knew, and worse, my parents knew, this "teacher" was
motivated, not by the desire to educate or even "coach," but
to humiliate.

That coach is dead now. Perhaps his personal Hell
involves burial in severed frog parts and an eternity of
summer diarrhea.

He wasn't, of course, the only stupid adult in Kentucky
and certainly not the only stupid teacher in the world. But he
was stupid. He is the one I think about whenever I worry
that I might have been unfair to one of my own students.
For the last decade of my teaching career, I made much
the same speech to each class on the final day of a school
year. I thanked my students for all that they brought to my
classroom and begged their forgiveness for any awkward or
stupid thing I might have said or done. "Forgive me, for
your own sake," I advised. "When you are well over forty,
you don't want to be telling a bored therapist that you still
hate one of your high school teachers." Perhaps I should have
begged them to resist any urge to write a memoir.

Puberty arrived, late and cruel. My freckles gave way
to tiny pimples that flared into zits the size of sunflowers.
Mother consulted Aunt Chris who recommended an astringent

soap that smelled strong enough to help but didn't. I felt crusty. Insulting the hormonal injuries, a cold sore erupted on my lip, the hideous lovechild of stress and a wandering virus. As I rounded the door into geometry class, smart-jock Paul, not generally one of the scary ones, announced for all to hear, "Hey, Dearinger, your syphilis is showing."

Thanks, Paul.

Better than "Summer diarrhea."

High school reunited me with Jo Rita Smith. Sort of. The years since the first grade and my forbidden kiss on the careening school bus had been kind to her. She was still pretty and petite, but now she was also very smart and grandly aloof. I suspect she was a bit shy. On the day we received our sophomore yearbooks, I spotted her—on the school bus. History should have taught me not to initiate contact with Jo Rita on a bus. Still, I was determined to have at least one other *girl*, one actual female, other than teachers and the dear Mouse, sign my yearbook. I once more lurched across the aisle to Jo Rita. She sat with straightened back and ankles crossed, her blue uniform sweater buttoned across her un-mouse-like chest. I spoke. No, I *squeaked.* A male mouse. I asked her to sign my yearbook. She said nothing, but she did smile, regally. No eye contact. No display of teeth. Just a tight-upturning of the corners of her lips. She was polite. She took my yearbook and opened it. Ignoring the pen that I offered, the one with the chewed shaft, she drew out her own pen. She paused, she pursed her lightly-lipsticked mouth, she wrote, she stopped writing, she closed the yearbook, and she handed it back to me. She still looked beyond me, not quite at me. I returned to my seat, delirious with anticipation. As the bus rolled off and bumped down South Broadway, I slipped a finger into my yearbook and opened it to the autograph page. There, in neat cursive, prominent and not to be missed by anyone who ever glanced at that page, still not to be missed to this day, Jo Rita had written, "To Kevin, whom *I don't really know.* Sincerely, Jo Rita Smith." The true humiliation was that strategic "whom."

The high school halls were thickly crowded between classes. All those boys and all those girls with books stacked on gender-appropriate anatomical areas, jostling for space, rushing to the bathroom if brave, or for a smoke if defiant, hoping for physical contact and terrified to touch another body.

I knew that Sandy Mudd was a nice, "older" girl, but I did not *know* her. One day, in the mobbed hall, she stopped me, and asked if I were "David's little brother." Yes, I said, in a timid pip. Sandy presented her right elbow at my eye-level and asked me if the patch on the sleeve of her uniform sweater was coming unstitched. Begun as Catholic thrift, elbow patches had become something of a stylish trend for the fashion-starved schoolgirls who loathed the sour discipline of uniforms. Tentatively, I touched Sandy's elbow patch, turning her arm gently, despite the crowd, to inspect a few dangling threads. *Slam.* A hard hand smacked into my head, stinging and inflaming my left ear. When my eyes regained focus, Sandy had fled the scene. The smiting hand belonged to Sister Richard Marie, Dean of Women. Her face contorted with outrage, "Dick Marie" bellowed, "Don't you ever, *ever,* touch a girl *there ever* again!"

There? The elbow? *Ever again?*

With a few exceptions, Sister, I didn't.

The assigned reading in my high school English classes offered little promise for the future. We read *Red Badge of Courage*—a grim world of doomed young men and death. We read *The Odyssey*—heroic he-men and seductive nymphs. We read Chaucer and Shakespeare, suitably expurgated for Catholics. For reasons of frugality—the school had dozens of free copies of the script—we read the creaky old melodrama *The Bad Seed* aloud in class. Sister Mary Dennis asked me to read the role of pig-tailed Rhoda Penmark, the cloyingly

sweet little girl who kills her rival classmate and a handyman.
What was that otherwise intelligent teacher thinking? It was a
co-ed class. She did not have to pick *me* to play a murderous
little girly-girl. Then she asked the most threatening bully in
the class to read the part of Rhoda's father.

Through gritted teeth, my steady tormenter growled,
"What will you give me for a basket of kisses?"

"A basket of kisses?" I cooed in coy return. "Why, I'll
give you a basket of hugs!"

This performance should have killed all my theatrical
ambitions. I am still surprised I was not killed, then and
there, by my raging scene partner.

We read a better drama, the novel *Great Expectations*.
I loved Dickens. I understood Pip's frustrations with his
hometown, but I think I saw more of myself in the reclusive
Miss Havisham. At home, again aloud, I read her passionate
definition of love:

*"I'll tell you," said she, in the same hurried passionate
whisper, "what real love is. It is blind devotion, unquestioning
self-humiliation, utter submission, trust and belief against yourself
and against the whole world, giving up your whole heart and soul
to the smiter—as I did!"*

More smiting!

Is it any wonder that when love arrived, I barely
stood a chance? By all rights, I should be spending my days
and nights in a dark and dusty room, partially veiled and
clutching an unworn shoe, with my Swatch-watch stopped at
twenty minutes to nine.

Some days, I think I might yet come to that.

Shakespeare offered clearer romantic resolution, if
only of a tragic variety. Zeffirelli's *Romeo and Juliet* was new
when I was in high school and became my favorite film. I
could already recite most of the balcony scene; it had been
an early vehicle with my star puppets. J. T. Tiger had been a
good Romeo. Mercifully, his red dress rendered him wrong

for Juliet. Juliet was played by a piece of fabric wrapped around a pencil, yarn for hair, with her girlish figure defined by cotton stuffing and rubber-bands.

Zefferelli's film was all color and texture and youth and passion and perfect skin. No one's syphilis was showing. The language, hot and bawdy, seemed to fall out naturally. I returned to the unabridged dictionary with happier results. Shakespeare became my more-certain entry "Into Manhood."

The sex in the film was tender and beautiful. It was the Sixties. The camera lingered long over Romeo's hairless chest and bare buttocks and offered a blurry flash of Juliet's full-ripened breasts. Few of us had seen such things before in a film. Or anywhere. The shock was a pleasant one. It felt good.

There were questions.

Did they or didn't they?

Had the young lovers actually "done it?"

Their nudity suggested that they had kissed *without pajamas*, and surely more. They were *in a bed*. They had "slept together" and faced the morning-after with looks of sleepy satisfaction. One of my English teachers, not even a nun, but a *lay* teacher, was furious with the film. Romeo and Juliet had to die virgins, she insisted; *that* was their true tragedy as Shakespeare intended it. I worried that such a fate would be *my* tragedy, but I had read the play and knew that R. & J. must have gone all the way. Even J. T. Tiger could see that, and he had only one good eye. Shakespeare did not kill off his young lovers until they had enjoyed the physical pleasures of the flesh.

Or were they the "sins" of the flesh, after all?

Even in fair Verona, sex did seem to lead rather quickly to death. Poison and a dagger in its human sheath. More Liebestod.

Years later, I worked with the actor who played Friar Lawrence in Zeffirelli's film. He told this story: the director, worried that his innocent young actors were too formal with each other, arranged a weekend assignation for them at a villa on Capri. Left on their own, nature took its course. At least according to the old actor's story.

My English teacher would have been shocked.

Romeo had Juliet, and Juliet had Romeo, at least for a few hours. At some point, I acquired a high-school girlfriend.

I had taken a girl to a dance in my freshman year. Daddy drove us in Mother's virginally white station-wagon. Becky and I danced a bit and talked very little. Her hair chose that night to go frizzy, and I was shallow enough to worry that she might be less cool than I was, although I knew that was unlikely. What turned out to be "uncool" was that I had asked a girl from another school, from another county. I had, of course, been forced to ask outside the sphere of my reputation. She was a nice girl, too, the first of not many but several "nice girls" I would get up the nerve to ask to go out somewhere with me. Lord knows I would never have asked them to stay *in* with me.

In my junior year, I "dated" a freshman girl. She was smart and pretty, with beautiful skin, like Juliet. She was also nearly as tall and nearly as thin as I was at the time. The school wags joked that when we walked down the hall together, we looked like the number eleven. 11. Laura was also as innocent as I was. We never kissed, but we did hold hands. I liked her, but she must have known something was not working in her favor. I ignored what I could. So did she. When she asked another boy to the Sadie Hawkins Dance, I pretended outrage, but I was relieved. I knew, somehow, that I had no right to be possessive or jealous.

Swimming once more out of the school-pool, I took a girl from my eighth-grade class to the Junior-Senior Prom. Plushly female and no-one's-fool, Jane was way ahead of me and far beyond. She was also in love with my brother. It was his Senior Prom. My rented tux was too small. My trouser hem fell well above my ankles—flood-pants. My wrists jutted beyond the sleeves of my boy-sized jacket, and I had a pimple on the sharp edge of my left cheekbone. Jane, bless her, was gracious. She always was. I adored her, in my way. I still do and always will. In my way.

These dating games went on into senior year. If I never told a lie, it was only because I didn't quite know the truth. I took good, kind, and safe girls to crowded dances. I presented my dates with wrist corsages and ran around to open car doors for them. We had dinner at The Little Inn or "The Club" and ordered *chicken cordon bleu*. Sometimes, we doubled with other couples who disappeared into dark corners and could not be found when it was time to leave. *My* dates were always home long before their curfews. Mothers liked me. Fathers shook my hand with a firm grip. I lowered my voice in conversation and lowered my head when asked about the current season in sports.

"*Go, Cats!*"

Even then I was aware that my speech patterns, clipped and tight, were not quite *right*. I said "cats" in one syllable, strong consonants and short vowel. Many Kentuckians elongated the word, stretching it out like a lazy feline in the hot sun.

"*Go, Ka-utts!*"

At some point, our high school's religion department, damaged priests unfit for parish duty, full of psychological ticks and traumatized tocks, decided to address S-E-X by all but its name and to attempt (Sex) –in muttered parenthesis—Education. I am sure they thought they were cruising along in the fast lane of the late Sixties, "Modern-as-Tomorrow." Groovy, Father, groovy. The nuns in the English department rocked with knowing laughter. No "foolish virgins," they. With a small shock, I realized that beneath their vows of obedience, they were fully cognizant of the ineptitude of their male religious colleagues. By then I knew that such incompetence was not so very difficult to recognize. Stupidity was not hard to find at a Catholic high school in Kentucky in the late Sixties. Alone or with others

Our priests rented a "sex-ed" film and offered it in gender-separate screenings. "Give us a full report," demanded my English Department nuns. With conspiratorial delight, I detailed for them the film's humorless solemnity. It had attempted a lesson on sexual anatomy by offering slow-panning shots of Michelangelo's "David" and the "Venus de Milo," zooming to close-ups of the statuary, which then rotated on screen in an arc of creaky animation. An apt metaphor for the Catholic vision of appropriate feminine desire, poor Venus did not even have arms. On-screen, the statues turned face to face and approached each other with marble carnality, but just before the moment of conjoined ecstasy and certain rocky rubble, the classical male and classical female were transmuted. David became a cylinder. Venus became a square box. What followed was unspeakable. It certainly colored my understanding of Art History.

All around me, however, sex was the Word Made Fleshy. High school sex was talked about in corners, performed in corners, and refined in the back seats of first-automobiles, oiled and shining with paste wax. Carburetors and "reputations" sputtered.

Fashion telegraphed interest. Girls with teased hair, militant brassieres, and too much makeup caused a stir. Boys hitched their jeans, strutting and adjusting nature. Everyone longed for a signal that could be understood. Reputations acted as open codes. Some boys were "just wild." Some girls were "easy." Like Romeo and Juliet, some went "all the way."

"Girls," of course, had the worst of it. Rumors and whispers. Mothers closing doors for private talks. Rolling up the skirt-waist when leaving the house and dodging the nuns who, with virginity stapled onto their lives like a wimple on plastic doll's head, had been set up to guard the sexual purity of the libidinous daughters of *Peyton Place*, Marilyn Monroe, Jane Mansfield, and, hybrid of horrors, beautiful *and* smart, Jane Fonda. From time to time, a modest and virtuous co-ed disappeared from school and went to "stay with relatives." At the Crittenton Home.

"Really Bad Mono."

There were more mixed-parties, to be sure. At sweaty sock-hops, fascinated on-lookers formed a wall around an advanced couple, allowing them to dance the forbidden "Gator" without interference from the frazzled, somehow jealous chaperones. On the fringes stood the innocent and the uninformed, the chivalrous, the devout, and the utterly terrified. I was perfectly happy to "leave room for the Holy Spirit."

Dominic Savio took Maria Goretti to the dance at the gym.

I knew "good girls," and "good girls" did not ask too many questions, especially with "good boys."

I apologize to them, one and all.

By the time I left high school, I had ways of talking to girls, now women, and of being comfortable in their presence. My manner did not fool the sharp-eyed.

"He's been 'round women too much."

Boys, now men, still made me uneasy. They all seemed to know more than I did. They seemed suspicious and impatient with my "pretended" innocence. It was not pretense. "Kevin?" said a high school acquaintance, "Oh, he's basically nice."

Basically.

Many of my slightly-older cousins were about to become parents, one way or the other. My sister married a football-playing, former Future-Farmer from the county high school. They eloped before sunrise on a winter's morning, car lights in the dark, approaching in mystery, departing in grief. Before my sister left, we said goodbye in the upstairs hall. She cried. So did I. Mother curled up and shivered on the living room sofa, unable to speak. Mother could stand anything, except the idea that her children were growing up.

Most of my days, I was alone. My brother was somewhere in his own solitude. He had understandably tired of having a little brother clinging to his social coattails and shaken me off.

I read everything. I watched old movies on television and knew all the film stars of the Thirties and Forties. I knew all about the careers and manufactured personalities of Katherine Hepburn, Cary Grant, Joan Crawford, Clark Gable, Vivian Leigh, and Bette Davis. I thought *Gone with the Wind* and *Rebecca* were the greatest novels and the greatest films ever created: sentimental romantic fantasies. I still listened to original cast recordings of Broadway musicals, sang along, and, in the privacy of my room, pretended I could dance. I wore the finish off the ash-board floor. I punished the parquet.

Dancing in the dark.

CHAPTER NINE

BLACK MYSTERIES OF BEING

This chapter skates on the very thin ice of partial knowledge and woeful ignorance. It is the best I can do for now. I feel uncomfortable in my pale skin when I try to write about race. I have mentioned grandparents, parents, siblings, aunts, uncles, cousins, and schoolmates, but always there was Arnetta, full of wisdom, full of shock, and full of life.

Arnetta was an African-American woman. After the birth of my brother, Mother felt overwhelmed. Barely fifteen years old, Arnetta came to "help with the ironing." She stayed to help with everything. She was never a "housekeeper," and had we called her a "maid," she would have hit us "in the head with a brick." Her expression.

For over sixty years, Arnetta was my mother's best friend, a Southern cliché, *Miz Daisy*, *ma'am*, but no less true for that.

Arnetta was also *our* best friend. Always. Like Aunt Chris, she was full of information that could not come from Mother or Daddy. She taught us to giggle at those portions of life that our parents pretended to ignore. Rather than avert her eyes from human foolishness, Arnetta would point and laugh, too honest for pretense.

We had a big white station-wagon and a green truck. Arnetta drove a nail-polish-red Impala with enormous fins and a liquor bar in the backseat.

Arnetta had *boyfriends*. They had names like

"Horse" and "Shank." When she married, late in life, her husband's name was William, but everyone called him "Dick."

Horse, Shank, and Dick.

At least, we knew what she liked.

"Don't be nasty!"

We called her "Arnetta," but everyone else knew her as "Peaches."

"Arnetta, why do they call you 'Peaches?'"

(I asked this again and again, because I loved the answer.)

"Arnetta, why do they call you 'Peaches?'"

"'Cause I'm so sweeeeet."

Arnetta and Dick were only married a few years. When he died, two ministers preached at his funeral. The first was all Hellfire and Damnation. He pointed to a funeral guest in the front row and chided him for not coming to church on the previous Sunday. There would be a day of reckoning, he warned, terrible to behold and not to be avoided. The funeral parlor grew tense. The second minister was gentle, a relief, it seemed. A Fundamentalist variation of bad-cop-good-cop. Arnetta had not had much time with Dick, he told us. And death can come quickly, without warning. "Now," he said in a comforting voice, "Arnetta wakes up in the night, missing Dick. Wanting Dick. Looking for Dick. Needing Dick. Smelling Dick."

My sister was sitting next to me at the service, and our reaction to this gentle observation did little to underscore our personal dignity. We grieved for our friend's loss but had she been sitting with us, I think I know what Arnetta's reaction would have been.

"Well, excuse the hog, 'cause the pig don't know no better!"

When we were very small children, Arnetta took us with her when she had her hair done. The beauty shop was on Third, near Race Street, in Lexington's most populous "negro neighborhood." We sat on the floor, waiting for her, in a room full of African-American women. Curls and conversation relaxed. Hair burned and "behaved." The ladies chattered and gossiped of men and sweet-sweet loving. They talked freely to each other about who had "big ol' titties" and who had a "big ol' bee-hind."

We were shocked.

We were thrilled.

"Black" music defined a world alien to our whiteness. We had Paul and Paula wanting to be "ma-a-ar-ied." *They* went to the "Chapel of Love." We knew that a good girl had to wait until it was "Judy's Turn to Cry," and that a "bad girl" might run with the "Leader of the Pack," but that there would be retribution and carnage out on the Karma Highway. When Carla called Otis a "Tramp," however, Otis made no apologies and even boasted of his wayward ways. Carla fussed and fumed but didn't really seem to mind. Their fight was sure to end horizontally. We had Elvis and the Beatles. We also had Edie Gorme and Giselle Mackenzie, shedding tasteful tears in tasteful torch songs.

They had Billie Holiday. She cried blood.

They shared Diana Ross and the Supremes with us, but Little Richard stayed dangerously all *theirs*. Sinatra could swing, ring-a-ding-ding. Little Richard tore notes to shreds and scattered them in his own time. There were rumors that he was "queer."

Had to be.

"Too strange, even for a black guy."

We had Alan "Mudah-Fadah" Sherman and Andy Griffith confessing that "whut it wuz wuz football." Humor as pale as our faces. The black community knew the comedy recordings of Redd Foxx and Moms Mabley.

The Lexington newspaper segregated African-American news in a back-page column called "Colored Notes," and, as a matter of policy, its editors suppressed coverage of the civil rights movement. Local protests went unreported, all in name of public safety and in collusion with white community leaders. In Versailles, the courthouse had race-designated water fountains, and the seedy downtown movie theatre had a "Colored Entrance" to the "Colored Balcony." We giggled when we heard that someone dark in the upstairs darkness had dropped a hot dog from the balcony and that a freckled white girl we all knew from school had picked it up and *eaten* it!

Or so we heard.

And we knew that Arnetta could not sit with us in a movie theatre.

The popular movies we saw had few African-American actors, but we all knew Sidney Poitier. Handsome, charismatic, and full of truth, he was hard to ignore. We saw him in *Lilies of Field*, singing with foreign nuns. No love interest; there to serve and enlighten. A man, but not all that makes a man.

Occasionally on television, black and white reception only, we saw an old movie with Stepin Fetchit or the sublime Bill Robinson. We loved and imitated Louise Beavers, the "funny black maid" on *The Danny Thomas Show*, who was scripted to ask, "Who dat say who dat when I say who dat?" (*High-larious!*) Diane Carroll brought earnest glamour to network television as Julia.

"A Credit to her Race," we were told.

How quickly good-intentions became condescension.

Our images of real people of color remained limited. Society prescribed that each race, the black and the white, maintain a scripted code of behavior when the other was present. NBC proclaimed programming in "Living Color," but we were not programmed to recognize the full spectrum of humanity. We went on living in black and white.

The local drug store sold a paperback edition of *Mandingo*. Well-thumbed copies circulated among pasty housewives, fascinated by steamy sex scenes, mistress and handsome slave in passionate coupling.

Meanwhile, everyone in town knew "the colonel's

children," the numerous offspring of an old, white "colonel" and his various African-American lady friends. He would bring his timid children into town and buy them candy. They had pale eyes and freckled skin of gold. No one said "biracial" or "mixed race." Just "one drop of black blood" made a child a "negro."

White adults would shake their heads and sigh.

"In these cases, it's always the children who get hurt."

Even then, I thought it probable that if the children were hurt, it was mostly because adults said stupid things like, "It's always the children who get hurt." Just who, I wanted to ask them, was doing the hurting?

Arnetta provided the leveling voice of reason in this maelstrom of sex and race. Later, when I was an actor-laddie in a play in Boston, I wandered into Filene's Basement and purchased a "Plantation Hat," blocked like a fedora, but with a wide, zoot-suity brim. *Powder-blue.* I wore it the next time I went home for a visit to Kentucky. *Cool.* Arnetta was there to meet me as I got off the plane. She looked at me. She looked at the hat. *Not cool.* "Take that fool thing off your fool head," she growled, "before your mama sees you. You look like a pimp!"

Arnetta was always quick to recognize a fool, and, if you asked, she would happily define the word "pimp" for you.

Years later, when two local businesswomen opened a cozy family café, the rumors went out that they were a "lesbian couple." It was the Nineties, and the L-word might at least be whispered. *And* they served quiche. My brother and sister met Arnetta for lunch at the café. She entered, sat, examined the menu, ordered, and then paused. She peered around to see who might be listening and hissed, "Which one is the *he* and which one is the *she*?"

Some conversations, we had. Others, we never did.

I have always wondered if Arnetta's experience as

a woman of color in a racially prejudiced society might have, on some points, paralleled my experience as a gay man in a persistently homophobic culture. It is not a discussion that time allowed us. I was too scared to "come out" to Arnetta, but when she stopped asking me about "girlfriends" and when I was going to marry, I knew she "knew." I worried, wondering if she would judge.

"Don't be nasty!"

Now, I will never know for sure.

When I was nineteen, a well-known national figure was arrested for "sodomy." I read about the arrest in the paper over breakfast and declared with college-boy nerve that I was surprised that a Kentucky paper would actually print the word "sodomy." Standing across the room by the kitchen sink, my mother voiced a faint, "Uh-huh." She came over and looked at the newspaper and at the *word*. "Kevin, honey," she asked very quietly, "what is sodomy?" By this time, I knew. I had looked it up and more. By some definitions, I was some sort of Sodomite myself. I was not, however, ready to share this knowledge with my mother. I remembered that in the eighth grade, we had read Bible stories and learned that the lustful residents of Sodom had propositioned the Lord's angels with un-angelic suggestions. Asked to explain the reason that those randy folks were destroyed by fire and brimstone, a very nervous nun had fumbled for a diversion and suggested darkly that sodomy was being "nasty" with *animals*. As we lived in a farming community, this seemed at the time as likely as anything else I had been told. By the time I was in college, I realized we had been duped, but "animal-sex" seemed a safer explanation to my mother than the truth, and so I followed the lead of the skittish nun. I lied and told Mother that the celebrity must have had sexual intercourse with an animal. After a pause for astonishment, she said, in a wondering voice, "Kevin, I grew up on a farm, and we *never* did anything like *that*."

Mother maintained vast reservoirs of innocence.

That weekend, Aunt Chris visited, and Mother shared with her big sister the misinformation I had imparted, more or less, on the topic of sodomy. They were in the kitchen; I was around the corner in the dining room, listening. I expected Aunt Chris to set her straight and expose my lie, but apparently, her Baptist expertise extended only to the more conservative traditions of men and women. "Oh," marveled Aunt Chris, "the things these kids learn in college!"

Then Mother repeated the whole story to a higher power.

"Arnetta, have you ever heard of such a thing?"

And, of *course*, she had.

"Sure," Arnetta said, "it happens all the time. There was a woman in Lexington who had puppies."

"Had *puppies*?" I interrupted.

Still a determined academic, even if one who had once listed Summer Diarrhea as a venereal disease, I explained DNA and the "incompatibility of species when it came to reproduction."

"I *know* what I saw," insisted Arnetta. "We found out where the woman lived, and we all drove out to her place. There were packs of male dogs circling her house, trying to get in on a good thing."

Horse, Shank, and Dick.

"Stop acting like a pig, hog!"

"Don't be nasty!"

They called her Peaches because she was "so sweeeet."

And she was.

Kevin Lane Dearinger

Chapter Ten

A State University

I had a choice. Two of Kentucky's small liberal arts colleges offered me scholarships, but only if I wanted to major in theatre studies. I wanted a more practical degree. Something really *useful*. I ended up at the University of Kentucky, majoring in English.

I knew all of the university's paths and most of its buildings. I had "grown up" there. My father was a professor in the College of Engineering.

I had, of course, seen the last of my intact foreskin at a campus urinal, but I learned that there were other reasons to fear the university's men's rooms. Patterson Hall and Old Anderson were bad, but, even worse, were the stalls at the Student Center, where I had spotted another "Vesuvius" on a wall of blue and white tile. The penis as volcano seems to be a universal Jungian trope.

"Go, Ka-utts!"

By reputation, however, the lowest circle of Hell was the men's room on the ground floor of the Fine Arts Building, near the music office. There, unlike high school, the stalls had doors, but privacy was for more than sneaking a cigarette.

Coming from a piano lesson in the Fine Arts building when he was fifteen, my brother stopped to use that downstairs men's room. Someone touched his ankle under the wall of the cubicle. He was terrified and fled. He told Daddy, and Daddy took him to the campus police. The chief officer was the father of a particularly vicious pair of twin gossips back

123

in Versailles. Papa Policeman told tales at home. His nasty daughters repeated the stories at the county high school. The cruelty of teenagers transformed my brother from victim to guilty party. Small towns, small minds, and large hurts. Innocents both, my brother and I had reasoned that someone had reached under the stall to try to steal his wallet, not his tender virtue.

When I began college, I had rarely spent a night away from family and did not own a pair of jeans. All my shirts were collared and button-down. I was still praying myself to sleep each night with the rosary in my hand.

It was 1969. This could not last.

I had never had a drink. In college, one was expected to drink. It was the manly thing to do. Throwing up your cheeseburger and onion rings along with rancid beer earned bonus points for virility.

Being drunk was also an excuse to express one's sexuality. I am now sure that part of my old obsession with *Dracula* had been Stoker's depiction of proxy-sex without guilt. The erotic bite of the vampire, the intimate exchange, was not consummated by mortal or moral consent. College inebriation pretended to offer the same guilt-free pass and trespass into the forbidden.

College sex sweated with Rebel Yell and Maker's Mark.

Later, it would be laced with the burn of straight-up Dewar's.

After a college party in the summer following my freshman year, a sturdy young woman invited me to a motel room. She stripped down to her underwear and jumped into the sagging double bed. *"Magic Fingers (Deposit 25¢) Massage."* She pulled the sheet up to her chin and asked me to sit by her. We kissed. I tried to do what was expected next. Oh, no, she said, kissing was as far as she ever went. Kissing in *underwear* might have been a high-point scorer on the high school virginity test, but I then learned what the guys meant when they called a girl "a tease." Unlike most *guys*, however, I was very grateful. Teasing was "joking," and I was happier to laugh at the joke than at my own terror.

At some point, I was roped into attending a fraternity dance. I distrusted the buddy-buddy frat boys, and my date was an uneasy sorority girl. We doubled with a couple that had been together since high school. My date drank heavily, Coca-Cola and bourbon, bourbon and Coca-Cola, and then just bourbon. Her breath became sticky, and her gait unsteady. After midnight, we four went to someone's borrowed apartment. The lights were low. The place smelled of stale beer, cigarettes, burned popcorn, dirty socks, and leaky plumbing. It was a "guy's apartment." The established couple headed for the bedroom, but before they left me alone with my date, they pulled out the mattress on a sleeper sofa in the living room.

"This is for you two."

My date and I were left alone. I sat on the edge of the lumpy sofa bed, both feet on the floor. My date drooped lumpily beside me. She slumped back on the mattress, turning her head to the side. She began to vomit. Streams and gushes. I helped her sit up. Her body was clammy with sweat and fear. I found a trashcan and held her head as she barfed up Kentucky's second-tier finest. Years later, after painful relationships and a botched abortion that nearly killed her, she came out as a lesbian. I hope she does not hate me.

What *were* we doing?

She was very nice and very smart.

So was I.

For a while, I called myself "asexual," a term I had found in my high school biology book as the frog parts flew. The boy who slept with his rosary and in pajamas buttoned tight up to the neck knew that this was not quite the right label. If pressed, I began to hint that I must be "bi." That was chic by the summer of 1970, and I had, after all, dated girls, if rarely women.

I did have "women" friends in college.

Kathy was secretly shy, but she covered it with clear consonants and a ribald vocabulary. She was breathtakingly intelligent and witty when the rest of us were just trying to make a fart joke. Kathy even told the best fart jokes. She wore purple with distinction and turned the air blue with alliterative profanity. She rolled out the words "smegma" and "scrotal" as if she were at center stage in a Congreve comedy. She taught me to swear, even if I could not bring myself to go any further than to call some offending something a "mother." I carefully omitted the f-portion of that vivid expression.

What the Freud!

Kathy came from a large Irish-Italian family. In Kentucky fashion, the men were quiet, and the women wondrously outspoken. Her Italian mother was a jolly conversationalist, full of good stories and throaty giggles.

Once, I waited in their knotty-pine den to take Kathy to a college party, a rare afternoon event. A great day-napper, she had overslept and kept me waiting. I waited for eight hours. I sat, ankles primly crossed, in an upholstered chair in front of a darkened television console. I could hear Kathy's mom in the kitchen, clattering pans and chatting with her other daughters. I was uneasy, not because I was kept waiting, as I was accustomed to that with Kathy and adored her too much to complain, but because on several previous visits, good old Shag, the family dog, had attempted to impregnate my kneecaps. Kathy's mom well remembered these canine advances, and she popped out to the den to assure me that Shag was safely cooped up in his backyard pen. "He'll be sorry to have missed you," she said, grinning. "He's been asking after you." She laughed, but then her face became serious, puzzled, flummoxed. She looked down at my belt, at my waist, then *below* my belt. "Patty," she shouted back into the kitchen to one of Kathy's sisters, "come out here and look at this boy's *pelvis.* He has a small pelvis for a boy. Not like my Bill. My Bill's got a *BIG* PELVIS. This boy's got a small pelvis." Patty rushed into the den. More shouts. Betty, another sister, came to inspect the wonder of my small pelvis. Still more shouts down the hall. Bill, the paterfamilias, stirred from his room. He was tall, *very* tall, and his pelvis was, indeed, impressive. The big-boned Irishman looked down on the hullaballoo with practiced forbearance. His wife indicated the size differences, his pelvis and mine, by stretching out her hands and then closing them together. It was the same gesture later used in television commercials for Preparation H, to indicate the effective shrinking of hemorrhoids. I *felt* hemorrhoidal. In the knotty-pine den, four people stared intently at my crotch. I might have preferred a vibrating bed in a private motel room with Shag.

I loved this family. They used the F-Word freely but never seemed vulgar. They laughed without caution-signs. They talked about sex, and it was clear that the parents enjoyed procreating. They liked sex, and their children knew it. In my experience, they were unique as parents and as a family, at least in Kentucky. It did not surprise me, however, that they were non-practicing Catholics, what the nuns called "fallen away." They had fallen away into nature and done so with relish. Irish and Italian but with no fear of moody bishops or fallible popes.

Kathy taught me many important life-lessons. She taught me to eat potato skins and how to make a gooey concoction called "Tuna Rarebit." Dignified cholesterol. She encouraged me to tell stories and embrace the foolishness of human behavior. She also taught me pride of intelligence and dignity of self. She taught me to laugh at myself, and she laughed generously at my stupid jokes. I roared at her wit. Daddy always said, "She's one of the smart ones." She was and is.

I had another "girlfriend" for a time, but she was also more of a friend who was female. Rachel told me later that she had been frustrated by my non-active "bisexuality." She also told me, long after the fact, if it was, in fact, a fact, that she eventually rendered up her virgin body to a young man she chose for the purpose because he looked like me. Rachel was always a fabled fabulist, but what a lovely compliment. In its way.

Again, I am sorry.

In the summer of 1969, just out of high school, I performed in a creaky musical. Rachel was also in the cast. So was a fuzzy-headed, recent college graduate named Lucky. He must have been four years older than I was, but to me, he just seemed older. We toured the show, and Lucky signed me up as his roommate. When we got to our room, I discovered that we were expected to share a bed, and late on the last night of the tour, he insisted on giving me a back rub. "Roll over now," he said in choked voice, "and I will do the other side."

Self-knowledge comes at odd times.

I fled to Rachel's nearby room and slept on her floor. By noon the next day, I had gone to confession. "Alone or with others" now made sense, even if not much had actually happened. I prayed that I would be forgiven for something I had not done. In my journal, I wrote of the "destruction of my soul."

I had understood what Lucky wanted, however awkwardly, and I began at last, to question what I wanted.

I never saw Lucky again and wonder what he remembers of this fumble if he remembers anything at all. I recall his curly hair and that strangulated request.

At the university, I had friends in the theatre department, housed in the Fine Arts Building, home of the terrifying men's room.

"Pee fast and don't go near the stalls"

Two of a triumvirate of theatre professors professed

quite openly that they were "homosexuals." They looked at men. They dined alone with men. At times they lived with men. They also flirted with, longed for, and seduced student actors. Or so I had heard. I was terrified of them and conversed with them only in respectful monosyllables, never making eye contact. The third professor, a married man, told me I had "well-turned ankles, good for Restoration comedy." I thought he might be hinting at something not theatrical. I was getting paranoid, but with cause.

Nervous to be in a department with a reputation for harboring "fags," some of the theatre majors made crude jokes. They mocked "musical comedy" as unworthy of manly dramatics and scorned a timid English major who wanted to "act." More terrifying to me, they pointed out and ridiculed groups of men on campus whom they had decided were "queer." They pointed out a crowd of laughing men that included my brother. I knew that they pointed out me. I seethed at the injustice, full of polite rage.

I just wanted them to like me.

Familiar need.

I was living at home, an increasingly stressful ordeal. My brother had grown more secretive and aloof. We had shared a room for many years but not since my sister had left home. Desperate for privacy, my brother had moved into her room before the ink on her marriage license was dry. Meanwhile, I was clutching my rosary, cuddling with the border collie, and listening to show tunes. "You Can't Get a Man with a Gun," no matter how many verses Irving Berlin gives you. You can't get him with a rosary, either. My nature was at war with my Catholicism, and I was miserable in the battlefield, my personal no-man's land.

For the first time, hardly the last, I tried psychotherapy. I took myself to the student infirmary at the university hospital. I told the receptionist that I was "stressed out," another of the great euphemisms, but I told the doctor on-call that I was gay. I think I said, "I am a homosexual." I know that, in free-fall, I babbled about wanting to fall in love. I acknowledged "certain urges," but I was still a "good boy." Love, real love, one person for another, might make what I was and what I wanted a kind of virtue to be winnowed out from "sin."

The good news from the doctor was that he was neither shocked nor censorious. The bad news, at least for my romantic soul, was his stern declaration that there was no such thing as love. "You don't strike me as stupid," he said, "and so don't fool yourself. Don't be dumb enough to think that sex is anything more than sex. Animals do it. We do it. Doesn't matter who or what we do it with. It's all the same. It's hormones and self-gratification, no more."

Too many uses of *IT*.

His prescription was a strong recommendation: "Move away from home. Get an apartment and get away from your mother. You are in this sinking boat because of your mother."

Freud has much to answer for, especially to mothers.

I never saw this doctor again. I don't remember what he looked like. I don't remember if he happened to be a young or old man. I do remember that his office had no windows. No way out. Like those high-school gym showers.

I grew up gay in the era of "blame the mother," but this never made sense to me. I lean on Nature, not Nurture. My mother loved me and did the best she could with the world she knew. If she behaved awkwardly as she realized she had two gay sons, her blunders were reactions, not causes. I had thoughts of my own about the nature of natural attractions. I agreed with the cynical doctor, however, that I needed to leave the nest, and Daddy helped me finance an apartment near campus. That is to say, he paid for it in full.

But I could not agree with that campus doctor on the topic of love. Love had to exist. Love between two men had to be possible. This, too, seemed only natural to me. It was my nature.

A year later, I tried another doctor. This time it really was "stress." I was overworked, with two jobs and a heavy course load. I was plowing through eight-hundred pages of required reading every week, banging out analytical essays on a cranky manual typewriter, and living on cheap spaghetti, powdered soups, saltine crackers, and triple-boiled tea bags. (Lipton's.) Arnetta told me I would be burned out, dead, by the time I was twenty-five. "You won't ever make old bones," she predicted.

My eyes ached.

Mother suggested I see her old psychiatrist, not a therapist, but a real M. D., a Freudian-couch-ink-blots-and-tranquillizers-by-the-truckload shrink. She had begun to see Dr. Meinkampf in her darkest days. He sedated her emotions and a good portion of her self-confidence with heavy doses of the latest drugs. I hope he listened to her, talked to her, cared for her. I hope that he eased her pain. I have, however, seen Mother's notes from her visits to this man. I think he played upon her insecurities to keep her in thrall to his Pez-dispenser. I think he enjoyed keeping unhappy women impressed with his power. I think of him now as a dangerous quack.

Charlatan!

On my first office visit, the good doctor would neither see nor speak with me. His rabbity nurse put me in a room for a two-hour test, "choose the provided answer that most closely matches your response" to a long list of questions and "fill in the bubble." The questions tended to be repetitive, prodding the same theme with slightly varied phrasing, as if determined to prove me wrong or catch me in a lie. Once I saw this pattern, I finished the two-hour test in forty minutes. No mention of Summer Diarrhea. I had no problem with the questions that pussyfooted around sexuality and asked if I had dreamed of, thought of, considered, fantasized, imagined, desired, craved, or beat a bongo at midnight for naked men. Hardly subtle, I thought, but not once did the form ask directly about my sexual identity. Multiple-choice offers tasteful limitations. I tapped on the door and gave my completed form to the surprised nurse.

> *"But you couldn't have finished it all."*
> *"I think I have, ma'am."*
> *"Perhaps you misunderstood the format?"*
> *"No, ma'am".*
> *"Skipped a page?"*
> *"No, ma'am."*

She told me to come back in three weeks. By then "the computer in Ohio" would have processed my results. The computer in Ohio promised to understand me.

Twenty-one days later, eyes still blurry with malnutrition and exhaustion, I returned. Doctor Meinkampf summoned me into his low-wattage office. He held a long, primitive printout from an early-days computer. I could imagine the flying punch-cards and whirling reels and blinking lights that had considered my answer bubbles and spit out an evaluation of my soul. I wondered if Meinkampf's brain operated with a similar whir and click. Dr. HAL 9000 with a red Cyclopean eye.

Dr. Meinkampf prefaced his reading of the printout with oily reassurances that I might have *misunderstood* the questions or darkened the wrong bubbles. I assured him that I had, to the best of my knowledge, followed directions, read the questions carefully, and answered honestly. I was, after all, an English major who had taken "Introduction to Psychology."

"Well," he intoned, "and don't be upset, mistakes are possible, no machine is perfect, and *don't be defensive*, but the computer suggests that you might have, just possibly have, please don't overreact, *homosexual tendencies*."

(Oh, hell!)

"I don't have *tendencies*," I answered, proud to be more precise than a computer. "I am a homosexual. In fact, I'm gay, and I don't have a problem with it. Not really. I *do* have trouble sleeping, and my eyes are tired. Could you just give me something to help me relax and sleep? Like you did for my mother."

"Whatever you do," he quickly replied, as if bitten by a weasel in drag, "never ever tell your *mother* that you are a homosexual. She'd never be able to handle it."

(*Oh*, answered my soul.)

"And here's the best advice I can give you," he continued, unasked. "Now just let me tell you a little story. I was a doctor in THE WAR, you know, and some of the guys in the barracks came to me to complain that there were two fairies in their unit. They said they thought those 'fellas' were looking at 'em funny in the showers. I called these two queers into my office and told them that I was on to what they were. I said to them that if they had to have those kinds of urges and needs, they should go out in the woods and just do it to each other and leave the normal guys alone. Just go out in the woods."

Oh.

I told him that if he would just write me a prescription for Valium, I would be on my way.

He did.

I was.

He prescribed ten milligrams of Valium, four times a day. The man was an idiot.

The next day I took the prescribed overdose at breakfast (saltines and a saucepan of boiled tea bags), borrowed my roommate's car, and started off to school. Three-and-a-half minutes later, a policeman stopped me for driving the wrong way down a one-way street. I showed him my bottle of pills, and he read the prescription. He shook his head, paused to look into my glassy eyes, and told me to go home and sleep it off. He followed me back to my apartment door and issued no ticket.

Driving the wrong way on a one-way street? The gesture had symbolic resonance for an English major.

The bottle of little blue pills, unused, stayed around until the night I used them all. Well, almost all.

I had seen the movies and read the books. I knew what was expected.

I tried to kill myself.

I was twenty-one, two months out of college. I was educated. I was inept.

It seemed suddenly that maybe love might be just sex after all, and that love and sex were what I would never get right. I had wanted to be a "good boy," but I never seemed good enough. I felt like the loser fish in the Starkist Tuna commercials. Poor Charlie the Tuna. Whenever he was on the hook, about to join the select, he would be tossed back to the bottom of the sea. "Sorry, Charlie." Starkist, and the rest of the world, it seemed, did not want "tuna with good taste, but tuna that tastes good." No one cared that I read the classics and listened to Beethoven and the blues. No one cared that I drank tea, not coffee. No one cared that I wanted to be witty and tried to be kind. No one cared that I was still trying my best to be a "good boy."

For a week before my big gesture, I started each day with a small bottle of orange juice and a walk in the woods.

"Just go out in the woods," the old charlatan had said.

I would hike a secluded trail, watching the morning vapor rise from the forest floor. There was particular clearing that I sought out; the ground there was covered with thick green moss, an image out of Arthur Rackham.

"Fairies," said the Freudian fraud.

At some point each morning, I would drain the last swig of orange juice, select a target, and then, with all my might, smash the bottle against a tree. Furious.

Bad Sex in Kentucky

"Eff you, Dr. Meinkampf, you mother-something!"

Mornings were a daze, days were hard, and then, one night, I took action.

I stacked six of my Billie Holiday albums on the spindle of my stereo and turned the volume down to a stifled moan. Yes, I needed a soundtrack. ("Gloomy Sunday," "You've Changed," "In my Solitude") I swallowed almost all of the leftover Valium, efficiently reserving one pill in case I needed it later. *Later?* I stretched out on my single bed, ready for another one-way street. I took a razor, a Gillette Trac razor, a small row of nippy blades, and made a few ineffectual hacks at my right wrist. I was too sleepy, too drugged, too unhappy to have much strength. As I sliced and saw the first sluggish flow of blood, I drifted off to sleep.

I woke up the next day.

I felt great.

My right forearm was a bit gummy, but I made it to a music rehearsal at nine and sang like a lark, a very relaxed lark.

I ended up with a small scar on my right wrist.

I have quite a few small scars.

As I once overheard the wise wife of one of my Kentucky cousins drawl to her sweet-souled husband, "Well, honey, of course you're damaged. We're *all* damaged."

Kevin Lane Dearinger

CHAPTER ELEVEN

GAY IN KENTUCKY

Even without knowing what to call it, I have always known, on some level, my sexual identity, or whatever we are calling it this week, but I grew up in a world that never stopped pointing out that I was "different" and that "difference" was "bad." I blamed myself because it was clearly my *self* that was "bad." For as much as this seemed unfair to a boy who wanted to be good, I knew that there must be a reason that I was called a "sissy" with such humiliating regularity. As far as I could tell, I was not as others were.

There were other terms and phrases. Sweetie. Swish. Fairy. Fruit. Pansy. Homo. "Been around women too much." Queer, of course, and faggot. Of course, these were not my words, but they were the words I heard, the words hurled at me, and the words that I resisted when trying to define my world. The dictionary was no help this time, at least not in defining my self.

I knew that whatever I was, it was intrinsic. Built-in, like bookshelves. That much seemed certain. Part of me stood defiant. I could play a few games for the world, but I was too stubborn and, at least on some level, too damn smart to pretend to fold into the expected norm. For a boy with low self-esteem, I had a remarkably clear and self-satisfied view of my own nature. A little knot of pride shook itself within me. I might be shy and given to daydreaming, but at my core, I was as sensible as a skillet. Cast-iron. The deeper shock, in fact, was discovering that I was not "the only one."

The words and the stories had always been around. The "others" had always been there. A local headline heralded the "Police Crack Down on Perverts," but I looked the other way.

"That has nothing to do with me."

But it did.

Other boys were as abused as I, some much worse. Their names were slandered on the side of a water tower, a public humiliation that never seemed to wash off. The girls spoke of them in scorn, and rough boys bragged of the insults they devised to punish Henry, "the panty-waist" and "mama's boy," and Harry, "the screamer," both public school boys. I met Henry and Harry at "mixed parties." I was terrified of them, afraid to be seen with them. Henry is now married and to a woman. Harry is also married and to a woman. I hope they are happy, but I hear that at least one of them "drinks." I wish I had known Henry and Harry better, but my cowardice would not have made me a very good ally.

And, yes, the boys I grew up with still used the term "panty-waist."

There were a few very public characters, the well-known "Homos." A downtown policeman's initials became a codeword among teenaged boys; keep away from his beat or he might try to "queer" you. Notorious Louie was a reason to avoid the Greyhound Bus Station. There was a whole block downtown where you did not want to be seen at night unless you wanted to "go in a car with a stranger" and maybe ask for money.

There was Henry Faulkner, an artist, renowned elsewhere in the wide world, but given the squinty-eye by the locals. A Kentucky country-boy who could convulse New York, Washington, and Key West with a flick of his wrist or tongue, he was a pressure-cooker of creative talent, brilliant and untouched by shame. He walked about downtown, consciously conspicuous with his halo blond hair and his steady companion, a goat.

The goat, a gothic touch, terrified me. Of course.

And everyone knew "Sweet Evening Breeze," an African-American orderly at Good Sam Hospital. Born James Herndon, he could be spotted as he "sashayed" down the street in a powder-blue lady's raincoat, with netted hair, pursed lips, and handbag clutched tightly to his bosom.

"Been around women too much."

"Sweets" was cultural chaos, and like Mr. Faulkner, fearless. Apparently, a visit to his home was an intimate rite of passage for the university's football players. Don't ask for details.

"Go, Ka-utts!"

Most of this underground gossip I heard when I was in college and roomed briefly with a chatty, chubby, self-loathing "flamer."

Flamer. Another of the words one heard.

Layers of judgment. Layers of dirt.

Male hairdressers, an accepted cliché, *flamed* with bottled brightness. They were expected to gossip, prance, preen, cavort, and "mince" for their adoring, high-coiffed lady customers. "Mince" was yet another standard code word. Male hairdressers were considered all of a kind; they *all* had toy poodles, *all* collected antiques, and *all* wore too much perfume, no, *they* all called it *cologne*. They lived in over-decorated rooms and tossed brilliantly colored silk scarves around their necks. They *were* toy poodles. They had young protégées, usually pretty blond boys from the mountains who became progressively blonder.

There were the men who *acted in community theatre.* Rumors abounded. Some of them spoke with phony English accents and wore pencil-moustaches. They drank *cocktails*, usually to excess. They never married. They looked after their elderly mothers.

"Never found the right woman."

There was a gay bar in Lexington.

"The Bar."

In other eras, it had been called The Gilded Cage
and The Living Room. It might just as well have been called
The Pit of Acheron. It was near the most popular downtown
movie theatre, but you should probably cross the street and
not walk by the door of The Bar. If you watched that door,
you would see men with unfocused faces who would walk
more swiftly as they approached the entrance, look as if they
were shooting by, and then suddenly side-dart through the
front door, swallowed up in a roil of stale cigarette smoke.
The local papers reported the police raids on The Bar, the
arrests, the names, the addresses, the damaged reputations,
the ruined lives.

The suicides.

And sometimes, the resistance.

There were rumors that Rock Hudson had met another
of the pretty Kentucky mountain blonds at The Bar and swept
him off to California and television stardom. More whispers, as
acrid as a burning cigarette filter wavering at the manicured tips of
spidery fingers.

"Quick! Look at your fingernails. It's a test."

A local girl was killed on her college campus. Outrage was
noisy, but gossip followed. Hints of a lesbian affair turned violent.

"Strangled with her own brassiere."

No one, of course, said *lesbian*, not until much later, and
even then, such talk was considered an *insult* to the murdered
woman and her family. Witnesses emerged to swear that she
was "devoted to her church," "sang in the choir," and lived
a "moral life," all to prove beyond the well-worn shadow of
a doubt that she could not possibly have been a lesbian. I
thought of some the tougher lady softball players and the
local lady gym teachers, living the grim stereotypes of their
time, unacknowledged, or dismissed into the realm of the
unspeakable. Still, if you listened, you might hear the coarse
snarl:

"That diesel looked at me funny!"

Words could spear my St. Sebastian heart. Walking down the street, innocent and unknowing, my heart bound in a rosary, I would hear "fag" or "fairy" and tremble. Did they mean me? The farmboy had slowed down his truck to screech "Faaaaaaaaaaag!" And "bad words" burned into my eyes from school desks and bathroom walls. That defiant "Fuck" on a lamppost.

Look the other way and quick.

Look up the words in the dictionary and hide whatever you think you know.

Daddy's hitchhiking story and Mother's admonitions. The army "queers" the doctor scorned.

"You know how they are."

Our high-school principal spanked bad boys with a wooden paddle. The "bad" boys dropped their trousers *and* their underwear, bent over the hard-breathing priest's wood-grain-laminate desk and took their punishment on bared buttocks. Only the jocks were in this manner entertained. The pumpkin-faced predator had no use for the physically underdeveloped boys. Years later, my sister heard the stories and asked if the priest had ever "tried anything" with me. No, I told her, he would not have recognized me in a police lineup. But I would have known *him*. In a police lineup. Or a nightmare. His was that old demonic face in the furnace-heat of my subterranean terrors.

But he did not even know my name; I did not play basketball. Meanwhile, I was pushed, shoved, and bullied in those high school hallways until the day that some self-imposed notion of chivalry demanded that I act.

Fate and alphabetical order seemed to put dough-faced Benny in a seat adjacent to mine in every class. The sullen boy tormented me for the first three years of high school. One day in an eleventh-grade English class, as the nun chanted expurgated Chaucer, he demanded that I give him my homework. I refused. He then turned his cruelty to Hilda, a shy, shaking girl who made me think of the sister in *The Glass Menagerie*. She rarely spoke and often cried. Noiselessly. As Benny teased and humiliated her, Hilda lowered her head in agony. Chaucerian couplets droned on as underscoring. Somehow, I found a voice. I warned Benny to stop and stop *now*. Mocking my outrage, he jabbed my hand with his Bic pen. I jabbed back at his attack hand with the sharp nib of my cartridge pen. (I was the sort who used a cartridge pen.) Benny's eyes hardened and nearly disappeared. The teacher noticed nothing, but the bell rang, and the rush out into the chaotic hallway began. Balancing on my left hip a binder and a full load of books, including the *Standard College Dictionary* that the rules said must come to every English class, I stepped into the surge of students.

Benny was waiting behind the door. I saw his fist. My books scattered. I braced myself, but I punched with my right arm and lifted my left knee to his crotch. I had never before this moment hit anyone. I was as terrified by my own violent defense as I was by the bully boy. Benny dropped his left hand to protect his groin. No, to protect his genitals. *Contact. And don't bother to call a foul.* I broke his thumb even as his right fist smashed my nose. Blood splattered.

I still have that *Standard College Dictionary*, baptized with my teenage blood.

The crowd parted before my Red Sea, and I made my way to the principal's office. I passed his secretary without a word and went into his sanctum-sanctorum without waiting. I made no effort to stop my blood from dripping on the white carpet. My voice returned. I would like to think that it did not break or wobble.

"I have been in this school for three years," I began, "and you have handed me prize after prize, but you don't know who I am, do you? What's my name? Do you even know my name?"

The priest sat silent, surprised and indignant. I could see the infamous paddle on the shelf behind his massive head, but I did not fear for a moment that he would try to use it on me. Not this day. Not ever.

"I know the rules," I continued. "If I'm in a fight, you're supposed to call my parents, send me home, and suspend me. But you are *not* calling my parents. I'll tell them myself what happened. And I'm going home now because I want to, and you will *not* suspend me. I don't want to hear about this again. Ever. And you still don't even know who I am, do you?"

Nothing more was said. I walked out. I took a bus to the university and waited to ride home with Daddy. At some point, my nose stopped bleeding.

I was not punished. I never saw Benny again. I told my parents some, not all, of the story. The school never contacted them. I heard later that the English department raised a glass or two to toast my rebellion. For years I thought how wonderful it was that some of my teachers rejoiced, but with time, I realized that their reaction only highlighted the fact that they had known all along of the abuse that came my way so regularly. They had done nothing.

This moment, this fight, somehow marks a watershed moment for me, but is this really how it happened? Was I really so suddenly resolute and direct? It is hard to remember what happens when the dam breaks, the glass shatters, and hell freezes over, when you have been hit and hit hard in the face and for once you strike back. But this is how I remember "the great fight." I only hope that my sudden bravery did, in fact, emerge, at least for that day, as I remember it. This memory is about all that makes thoughts of high school bearable.

It is a memory I still need.

But hitting someone, anyone, even a bully, shocked me. I still longed to be a "saint."

For several years I had actually imagined that I might become a priest. In elementary school, I had prayed to have a "vocation." Sister Alma Joseph, the guardian against mixed parties, was sure I had a "vocation." She gave me the statue of rosy-cheeked St. Tony. I was, of course, the head altar boy. My brother and I were usually the priest's attendants for the Tuesday night Novena to Our Lady of Perpetual Help. We were in charge of the incense. Novenas called for quite a bit of sacred smoke. We would hear Sister Alma Joseph cough in reaction to the incense; we waited for it. We giggled. We giggled on the altar. Finally, one night after the novena, Sister Alma Joe rushed to the sacristy to scold me. If I did not take greater care, she warned, my religious "vocation" would "fly." She turned furiously to my sniggering brother and demanded to know what had happened to *his* vocation. "It flew," he responded. By then he was already in high school.

Perhaps it was no coincidence that the years of my most intense religious yearning were the years that marked my slow progress through puberty. In the eighth grade, I interviewed with a Maryknoll recruiter who left me with a pile of pamphlets full of photographs of half-naked, starving *heathens*, that is, non-Catholics. Even then, I knew that "heathen" was another coded word for those who were excluded. I understood that I would always be, in some way, a "heathen."

Sometime that same year, when I was thirteen, I found myself committed to a retreat at the diocesan seminary in Northern Kentucky. I was to go for a week or a long weekend—memory wobbles here, as if punched in the face in a high school hallway—to stay at the seminary, with the seminarians, and with the resident priests. A retreat among men with men and only with men. Sharing prayers, meals, rooms, and showers with men. This was intended as a prelude to acceptance for training for the priesthood. Time lurched unsteadily towards the departure date for the retreat, and suddenly I found myself standing in my parents' driveway, looking at the closed car trunk. Inside the trunk was my small suitcase. All I had to do was get into the car. My mother was set to drive me the seventy miles to my "vocation."

As a priest. A *celibate* priest.

I felt a spiritual nosebleed.

No, I said calmly, I would not go on the retreat. No. Sorry, but *no*.

First bewildered, then angry, my gentle mother *snarled*.

"I wish you had never been born!"

(Ouch!)

I realized that Mother would have been proud had I chosen a religious life, but her reaction seemed all out of proportion to my offense. I had not seen this level of fury in my mother since the Fiestaware saucer had hit the yellow wall.

Entering the priesthood, of course, could have been the perfect public explanation for my not marrying. I could become "Father" without fathering children. Had I been ordained, Mother could have excused my being the way I was, whatever that was. She could banish "Blame the mother." At the time, she railed against my "hard-headed stubbornness." I was signed up for advanced Latin classes in high school, just in case I changed my mind and decided to embrace a religious vocation. I did not.

My vocation had flown.

The class of seminarians that might have claimed me after the eighth grade was the last such class of thirteen-year-old boys at that Kentucky priest-factory. The seminary's high-school level suddenly closed its doors for good. Or bad. A number of its ex-seminarians showed up at my high school. "Something happened" there, we heard, but the boys had been sworn to secrecy. The "something," it was whispered, had to do with "sex."

Extraordinarily uninformed, I wondered at the time how the students had managed to smuggle *women* into the seminary.

Meanwhile, I prayed for those who bullied me, said the rosary each night as I went to sleep, confided my innocent secrets to my puppets, and did not progress much beyond softball with a border collie.

In high school, the most popular euphemism, the primary "gay" identifier, was still "not-athletic." One lady looked at me with a well-intentioned pity and sighed, "Oh, you're just not sports-minded, are you?"

Oh, hell no, lady!

I had been hit on the head with that basketball when I was five and resented it. In the home movies of "the kids" jumping in and out of a driveway wading pool, I am the one who splashes into the shallow water, slips, falls hard, and comes up, bloody and crying, into the recording camera. Kentucky was full of white plank fences, and every kid I knew could balance and walk on the top rail, an expected childhood skill. I tried. I fell off and bit a hole in my tongue. I had been the boy hanging helpless on the chin-up bar in P.E. I was the one coughing blood at the end of the Presidential Fitness Test. I went to basketball games and cheered loudly for the success of the same boys who tossed me into lockers, put gum in my hair, and spit on me. I watched game after game and hoped that my pretense of caring would be enough, but I never quite figured out the rules of the game, the sacred Kentucky game. Hoops. I had my own hoops to negotiate, but I was decidedly "not athletic."

"Not sports-minded."

When the biology un-teacher was more useless than usual, he would cancel class and take us all to the gym to "shoot baskets." This made him very popular with some. There were a few of us, however, who were always sent off to the bleachers to watch. We were a "non-athletic" crowd. Hank, double-baited by acne. Languid Tucker. ("Tucker, tucker, bo bucker, banana-fana fo fu…") And sly-eyed Jerry, who all the girls "just *loved*" because he was a good dancer. The bullies chanted humiliating rhymes to his name, making me blush, and yet he seemed to look down on me.

There were others.

I later realized that most of those "non-athletic" boys in the bleachers were gay. That pea-brained coach was a world-class homophobe, but, apparently, he also possessed world-class Gaydar.

I am the only one of the bleacher exiles who comes to class reunions. When I last heard of him, the boy with bad skin was still living at home with his mother. The languid one is now a prominent local "bear," the gay, middle-aged, slightly pot-bellied, defiant version of "non-athletic." I see him, jubilant, every year at Pride gatherings; he wears a leather kilt and does impressive fund-raising for charity. Jerry is a retired dancer, who left Kentucky for five decades. "I got out as soon as I could," he told me recently, "and never looked back." Like me, he eventually came home. With understandable trepidation. He has, however, survived and prospered.

Others died young.

HIV-AIDS.

Timmy and Chuck had been my only two friends in elementary school, but to find them I had been forced to drop down a grade, to the class behind mine. We stayed friends, of sorts, when I went off to high school. When the gum was in my hair, I had the comfort of knowing I had two friends I could call when I got home. We seemed to understand the common enemy. When I was a sophomore at the Catholic school, my two friends were freshmen at the county high school. They scrambled to survive. They called and told me on the phone that they could no longer be my friend. I was not "popular." I was "not athletic." We had lagged behind with puberty, and when it caught up with us, we had no idea what to do. Insecurity needed a scapegoat, and I was it. "Very well, very well," I thought, hoping that meek acceptance of rejection and humiliation would earn me a plaster statue next to "Tony." I said my rosary and prayed for understanding.

I went to a cook-out hosted by the Catholic couple next door, a couple I idolized, although not by the end of that evening. They had invited the parish youth group, and so I was included. I wandered around, hoping to have a good time. I overheard pop-eyed Polly-Jean from elementary school, now a loud high-school sophomore, drawl, "Oh, Kevin. He has *no* personality." Blandly vicious, she continued over low laughter, "He has *no* friends." Our hostess, an adult, my *friend*, cooed in cruel agreement. (Yes, I am still angry.) Chuck, my erstwhile friend, was there, and he laughed at Polly-Jean's brutal judgment. He had a date that night, a bleached out, river-ratty girl named Ronnie. That "–ie" haunts quite a few Kentucky women. Ronnie called my parents' home with sad regularity, hoping I would answer the phone. When I did, she would shout, "Queer." Then she would hang up.

I left the cookout early and walked back home, next door. From my bedroom window, I could see the barbeque fire and the flickering silhouettes of those I had fled. I could hear them laughing. I prayed. Then I sat at my desk and tried to organize my thoughts on loose-leaf paper. "God's world is beautiful," I wrote, and "and He will make everything alright." I made a masochistic list of all the sorrows I felt. I catalogued the faults of those who hurt me, but all their flaws, I concluded, were mine as well, only worse. "I know it is wrong, but I want to die," I wrote.

I didn't die or even try. Not then, anyway.

I had a border collie there to save me. Again.

I might, however, have taken Polly-Jean's observation

about my lack of personality as a compliment. Personality was a popular word in school, along, of course, with popularity, but in Kentucky "real men" were, as far as I could tell, not supposed to have "personality." Personality might include wit, and wit was forbidden. Men could make dirty jokes, not witty ones. "Fuck" and "Pussy" got a sure laugh, in any combination. The lines were drawn. Any comment not laced with a reference to genitals or the elimination of body waste was a possible offense against the code of masculinity.

Timmy and Chuck went their own ways. I rarely saw them. Chuck attended every sporting event he could find, pumped up at a gym, shoved his voice down into a lower range until he sounded like the late Lauren Bacall, and had a few boyfriends. He dropped Ronnie when her roots began to show. Now, he is another fuzzy-wuzzy "bear." I hope he is well. I trust that my initial perception of his goodness was correct. He still goes to all the university's basketball and football games.

"Go, Ka-utts!"

Timmy was more vulnerable. He started to drink, moved away from home, and drank more. He partied with drugs and boys and went to bars. I called him once when I was in his adopted town. I had found him through the phonebook. He said he was not in good enough shape to see me, but he asked me to write to him and tell him how he could be gay and, at the same time, a "good Catholic boy." He was nearly forty. I wrote a long letter, telling him what I knew to be true. He was a good man, a decent man, and no church, no priest, no oppressive culture of hate could alter his goodness.

I have no quarrel with religion if it makes lives better, if it comforts the sacred human heart. I have no patience, however, with the religions of exclusion, religions of shame, religions of "my way or to hell with you." If you ask me if I believe in God, I will tell you that the answer is none of your business and that your ideas about The Great Divine are none of mine. The spiritual life of the individual is as personal as the secrets my parents kept about their honeymoon, as private as the stories I will never tell.

And yet, please note, I capitalize the name of the Deity.

God.

The Sacred Heart.

I never heard back from Timmy. A few years later, tortured by guilt and exhausted by HIV, he got drunk at a bar, hailed a cab, told the driver to stop on a bridge, and jumped. That is the story I was told, but I keep hoping that this was not how this tender-hearted man died. He deserved to be surrounded at the end by love and loving friends. He is buried in a Catholic cemetery. I visit his grave several times a year. "I am sorry," I say, but I am never sure what all that "sorry" should include. Remorse cuts deeper every year, exposing the limestone palisades of love undone.

When I leave the cemetery, I am never moved to head to a church. More regret. More stone.

I had one straight guy-friend in high school. Joe was a champion runner in almost every track and field event. He trained. I took long solitary walks at twilight in the back pasture of my parents' five acres. Sometimes, without thought, I would begin to run, tearing around and around and around the field, as fast as I could, fast enough that thought almost stopped. I was just two thin legs, a heaving pair of lungs, and a stronger heart than I had imagined. Several times, on moonless nights, I stripped off my clothes and ran naked around the dark field, around and around in frantic circles.

"Nek-kid as a jay-bird."

Back at school, Joe, brave enough to be my friend, would suddenly say, as I imagined *real* boys must often do, "Let's race. On y'r mark. Get set. Go." And the two of us would run to a shouted designation or until one of us stopped. And, to my surprise, I sometimes won. I still suspect that he slowed down to let me. He really was that generous, that kind, and that good.

And yet, when I finally admitted to myself that I was gay, I could not bring myself to see him. I was afraid that Joe would think I had been lying to him. I saw him at a high-school reunion, married, happy, unchanged at heart, with the old easy smile and uncomplicated honesty. We had not talked in forty years. Always kind, Joe suggested we get together and have a drink or lunch. I haven't called. I am still afraid of letting him down.

In college, I was still listening to recordings of Broadway musicals. I had an ever-growing collection of show albums, carefully alphabetized. I knew every song from a number of musicals, famous and famously obscure. I still made up dances in my head and shuffled my feet on the floor, smiling broadly in what I imagined was the musical comedy manner. I still liked Ethel Merman and could sing at great volume with true pitch. Merman was my first voice teacher. Formidable. I thought about ways of "selling a song." I did not know anyone else in Kentucky who thought about "selling a song." It was something they did in movie musicals. I could tell from the energy that flew out of the cast recordings that it was something that still happened in a Broadway musical. I wanted to "sock it out to the back row" and "hold for applause." Maybe even cheers. I longed to "strut my stuff" in a musical.

I later learned that a character in a musical sang when there was no other way to express a huge emotion or a surge of revelation. That may, in fact, explain more than singing in a musical. I was nearly bursting with unexpressed emotions and stifled revelations.

Kentucky was a straight play. I needed music.

In 1969, Musical Theatre had led to a closing-night backrub and mumbled guilt in a dark confessional. In June of 1970, it took me to a summer stock job at an outdoor theatre in a state park, down in the mountains. I had auditioned on a whim and signed the contract only after flipping a coin.

"Heads, I head out; tails, I tail behind."

Heads won. I was not sure I would.

I held on to the signed contract for a few more days. My parents expressed concern but did not explain why. I prayed, and after Sunday Mass, I accepted the decision of the coin-toss. I stepped to the mailbox on the corner by the church and mailed my first theatrical contract.

Four shows, "as cast."

Adventure.

I packed my pajamas and my rosary. I spent my leftover high-school graduation money ($300) on my first car. I bought it from the salesman father of a high-school friend. I proudly washed and vacuumed my '63 Corvair, with its AM radio and engine in the back. Under the front seat, I found a stack of extraordinarily raunchy pornography.

My friend's father's porn.

An omen to turn back or re-flip the coin?

"Run, run, run, run, run-away."

On the appointed day, however, I set out under a hot-blue sky on the two-hour trip into the Kentucky mountains to the outdoor theatre that promised me the music of Jerry Herman and Stephen Sondheim, live on stage. As I pulled onto the Mountain Parkway, the air began to cool. Then, with a solid thump, a robin crashed into the grille of my Corvair. I stopped and used a Kleenex to remove a small spray of blood and the feathered corpse.

Another sign.

Hope was obviously *not* the "thing with feathers."

Several miles later, the engine in my sex-and-death-tainted car blew up in oily black smoke.

Yet another sign.

I had read *The Return of the Native*. Now, I had wandered into a Thomas Hardy novel. Relentless Fate.

Personified and Southern-fried. Everything but a dead mule.

Alarmingly, I was not alarmed.

Instead, I sat on the side of the road, admiring the valley view and nibbling Nabisco sugar cookies, ringed on my little finger, until a station-wagon full of other traveling actors stopped to rescue me. They remembered me from the auditions. They took me to a fly-blown service station, where I bought a full case of oil, and then returned me to my Corvair. Stopping every few miles to pour another quart of oil into my smoldering engine, I pursued my destiny further into the Kentucky mountains.

I made it to the theatre. Everyone there seemed so sure of themselves. They were so insistent on their talents. So loud. So sophisticated. They ate cheese that was not Velveeta.

I had headaches in rehearsal.

I slept in the dressing room with nine other young men. I had a top bunk, in a row of five, double-stacked, army-issue cots. The beds were no more than two feet apart. I wore my buttoned-high pajamas to bed and said my rosary. All through the night, the lights in the communal shower at the end of the room threw the beds and the boys into silhouettes and shadows, a half-dream.

One night, twenty-four inches away from my sleepless form, two young men in the next bunk had sex in the dark that wasn't dark enough. They whispered passionately to each other. To be fair, it was not sex. I know now that it was making love.

I clutched my rosary tighter.

If I got up early enough, before any of the others stirred, I could find a few moments of privacy in a corner of that tiled shower, curtainless at the back of the dressing room. One morning, I stepped under the shower, the hot water steaming in the cold dawn air. As I passed a washcloth over my chest, I discovered something new. I had a chest hair.

My first. Just one. Reddish-blond against my pale sternum. I soaped up my chest, shampooing my single chest hair. Proud. Manly. Ready for the world. I rinsed my body and plumped up that one hair.

It broke off and ran down my leg.

Then down the drain.

Another omen?

Mother came to visit, and we spotted the couple I had seen and heard make love in the communal dark. The two young men were boldly holding hands on a country road in the Kentucky mountains. This was the summer of 1970. "Oh, they're *lovers*," I explained to my mother. I thought I was being grown-up.

Mother looked away and said, "Oh." A long silence followed.

Five years before this, the summer before I was in the eighth grade, I had picked up a controversial issue of *Life Magazine* at my mother's kitchen table. Its mostly-black cover announced articles devoted to the sinister mysteries of homosexuality. *Life!* One photo showed a man, face obscured, wearing cowboy and leather gear. My mother passed by. "Oh," she said cheerfully, eyeing this manufactured masculinity, "now, that's a *real* man." Then she saw the headline and the word "homosexual." Again, she said, "Oh." This time, the exclamation began softly and then trailed away. Her eyes went dull, and she moved away, silent.

In the summer following my musical trek to the Kentucky mountains, I worked in downtown Cincinnati and learned where the lady hookers lined up, standing about in short skirts, feathers, fur jackets, and thigh-high white boots. Mother again came to visit. "Those are prostitutes," I told her, as I drove her to lunch and we saw the ladies of the evening in the early afternoon. "Reeeeeally?" she said. "Prostitutes?" Mother made me drive around the corner and come back so that she could have a second look.

Not so the year before when she saw the handsome young men holding hands on the mountain road. Then, nothing more was said. There was no desire for a closer look.

"Oh."

Later that summer it all happened. The omens had appeared and then the event itself arrived.

It.

My journal knew more than I did. I had been writing every day in that journal since the summer before the eighth grade. I called it a "Journal" because "Diary" sounded too girly. On lined loose-leaf, I rambled and complained and tried to be poetic. "My life is out of control," I wrote in my mountain-summer of 1970, unconscious of the sexually-overloaded metaphor, "like a train rumbling through a dark tunnel."

More dark tunnels. More demons, unseen, but breathing near. More fear.

I finally got a small part of the "college boy" tradition right. I got drunk. More to the point, I was *made* drunk by an older man, a man with the power to fire me from a job I loved. He plied me with liquor as if I were a Victorian virgin, just so that he could paw at me in the back seat of his low, gray, filthy car. I passed out and woke up fitfully, with him on top of me. He smelled of unwashed clothes, cheap liquor, and greasy guilt. The guilt was infectious. He was a sad man, and he transmitted his sadness to me. An STD of the soul.

I am still not sure how much happened, certainly nothing that either of us could or should recall with pleasure. But it was enough. I do remember the Kentucky night air on my skin when he removed his clammy flesh. Several therapists have called what happened "rape." At the time, I actually thought that this kind of touching must be a token of love. It was not even an effort at honest intimacy.

It was, of course, about power. He was my employer. He could send me away in disgrace. Sensing his ugly advantage, he told me ugly things that scared me. Into my fear, he poured stories about his predatory world, even as he preyed on my neediness. He hissed half-revelations, secrets that he said he knew about my brother. He was manipulative, almost laughably so, and too devoid of style and decency to make what he did and said anything other than revolting.

I was stupid. A feeble conquest. I had allowed myself to be a commodity, to be used and bragged about. My rosary had not protected me from the vampire.

I don't remember how I got back to my bunk bed. I know I vomited. I know I showered for a long time, scraping at my skin.

The next morning, I met my visiting parents for Sunday Mass. Sin-sick and visibly groggy, hungover in body and soul, I prayed in incomprehensible phrases. When we made it to a restaurant for breakfast, Mother excused herself to the ladies' room, and Daddy asked, with concern, if I had been drinking. When Mother returned and Daddy went to wash his hands, she asked the same question in the same tone. Separately, I told them there had been a party. There *had* been a party. Separately, I told them that I had taken a drink and that it had not agreed with me. True enough. I told them each that the drink had been my first. It had. I did not tell them of the other "first." Had I done so, they would have whisked me home to a confessional and a shrink. They would have done the best they could with a son of the sort that society had educated them to abhor.

So I thought. So I feared.

How could I tell them something that might make them love me less or not at all? I felt certain that something was *wrong with me* and that I must not contaminate my parents with that wrong. There could be no comfort. No acceptance. No understanding. They loved me, yes, but they loved the boy they thought I was, the one I was supposed to be, not the young man I really was.

I remained silent and did the best I could. I knew all about silence.

I stopped praying myself to sleep with the rosary.

I went back to work, performing on stage with a barely controlled rage, desperate to be liked, eager to be somebody—anybody—other than myself.

The next year I met my first "big city" gay boys. That was the summer I worked in Cincinnati, which counted as a big city if you were from Kentucky. The hookers there were honest enough to look like hookers. I had my second summer stock job, and, again, a number of my colleagues were gay. Those Ohio gay boys assumed I was a "briar," a term I had not heard before that summer. It meant "hillbilly." My habit of going barefooted did not help. It was 1971. I was trying to be a free spirit. I wore a woven Tibetan sash instead of a belt. I finally bought jeans, with bell-bottoms fully-belled.

To those Ohio boys, I was also, to use their term, "fresh meat."

Only later did I discover there had been a bet as to who could bed the blond tenor first. It took all of three nights, a cheap spaghetti dinner, and a bottle of Boone's Farm Apple Wine. Again, the clumsy fumbling, the dirty feeling, the guilt on both sides. This time I tried to fumble back, but the experience remained ugly and sad. I felt far away before, during, and after the event. I also felt sick, and not just from the get-drunk liquor. Physical contact with my sloppy seducer was repellent. I had liked his intelligence and musical talent. I thought he liked me. I imagined that he would be as kind as he was gifted, but suddenly he could not look me in the eye. He never looked me in the face again.

He did, however, win the bet.

As must have been inevitable, I began to develop a thicker skin.

Just the thing what I did not want.

My inner voice took on an edge. What had been lyrical became cynical. Mother later told me I had lost my "soft, Southern ways."

I began to meet interesting young men.

And *interested* young men.

Men who collected early Streisand recordings, and men who actually listened to *later* Streisand. This, I would learn, was a meaningful distinction. The first was gay; the second was really-really gay.

Men who decorated their apartments with photos of Judy Garland and "stayed all night to sing 'em all" at Carnegie Hall. Add in Johnny Mathis, and the musical code was complete.

Men who imitated Bette and Kate and told Tallulah jokes, as if they were fresh.

Men who were alcoholics and not yet twenty-one.

A flamboyant Jewish man who carried a purse-like pouch and gave me his mezuzah, said he loved me, then moved to New York, became semi-famous, and seemed to recall me only vaguely.

An uneasy redhead who made me breakfast in his absent parents' luxury, high-rise apartment on a hill above Cincinnati, the "Queen City." I had never known people who lived in *nice* apartments.

An iconoclastic artist who called himself "The Virgin White," which was, of course, just what he wasn't. The Cincinnati phone company refused to play along and listed him in the directory as "White, T. V." For one of his art projects, The Virgin fashioned a phallic, over-the-shoulder, papier-mâché, vaudevillian's kiddie-car. He called it his "Penismobile." Outrageousness was somehow a necessity.

It was like falling.

It *was* falling.

Things happened *to* me.

I felt as if had no control over the situations into which I fell. The vampires were biting.

I was told that my Cincinnati director, an older man, liked blond boys and that I should let the old man have a little and keep him wanting more if I wanted to be cast in leading roles. I was nice to the "old man," who must have been nearly fifty, because he was a nice man, but I kept my distance. Terrified. His hair did not look real. Neither did his teeth. As far as the casting couch went, that was a game that I could never play. An actor I later knew used to say about sharing sexual parts in exchange for stage parts, "Only out of gratitude, never in anticipation."

I was determined to be grateful but "keep room for the Holy Spirit."

Years later, carpooling with other actors, riding back to Manhattan after a Saturday night performance in New Jersey, I heard a colleague speaking of me with great pity. "Poor Kevin," he said, admiring his own vulpine cheekbones in the rear-view mirror, "he just has his talent to rely on."

The other actors in the car nodded.

"Uh-huh."

In Cincinnati, in 1971, two years after Stonewall, I was enticed into going to "piano bars," those noisy gay bars in denial. There were perfumed women and perfumed men. I was always asked, "Is this your first time?" Once, I ran into my brother. We behaved as if we were in a Coward play and dazzled the Ohio boys by being cut-glass witty. Or so we thought. I was playing many roles, most of them more challenging than the eager, first-kissed boys I played on stage.

Somewhere, between the remnants of my Catholicism and the Sexual Revolution, between garbled gay traditions—*Get you, Mary!*—and rumors of Stonewall, between innocence and easy virtue, between hard facts and willful stupidity, I fell in love.

And Danny loved me back.

159

We stayed up talking late into the night, breakfasted on omelets at noon, and slept during afternoon movies, snuggled down, holding hands in the dark. It was a college affair, mostly carried on by long distance, by pockets full of change at pay phones, student-discount airline tickets, and daily letters on blue or beige stationary. I had never seen stationary that was not white. I had not known men who used "stationary."

Danny and I shared all our secrets and wore black turtleneck sweaters to cover our passion-bruised necks. No mosquito bites, no vampires, and no mixed parties.

Just us.

It began with fascination and insular devotion. It ended as such obsessive affairs must, but with love and no shame. At last, *no shame.*

I was very young, but the love I shared with Danny still resonates through my life, clarifying what is possible between two souls. Our passion gave way to a long friendship, years of honesty, and still no regrets.

And he died.

It was *that time* in gay history, in the history of our lives. "When it gets bad, really bad," Danny told me, "I won't call. I'll just be gone."

And so, one November day, the phone call came from someone else, someone I did not know. Someone who called him not "Danny," but "Dan." I went to his apartment and sat by the cold sheets of his unmade bed. His tender and exhausted body had been taken away. I sat there by myself, knowing that my gesture, my presence on a chair by an empty bed, was theatrical, self-indulgent. I knew that Danny would not mind, would not judge. I felt his still-loving spirit in that room. I feel it in every room, in every day, in every moment. I am grateful. He will always be The Possible.

Was it really love? Or do I cling so hard to the memory of Danny and what we were so briefly and so long ago as a reason to excuse my life of solitude? Has it been easier to claim a lost love than to admit that deep flaws and old traumas have kept me from long-term intimacy?

I believe that I have been loved and loved in return. Maybe that's enough.

I have been selfish. Still fearful that full-disclosure will bring alienation, I violently shove away anyone who delves too deeply into what I hide.

But when I die, I hope that I am still remembering the warmth of Danny's soft skin, the tiny vertical ridge on his lower lip, and the infinity of his eyes when they opened on a shared pillow and gazed at me and I gazed back.

This *must* have been love.

Perhaps it was only sentiment that became nostalgia. It is what I have.

I hold it, sacred, in my heart.

A Brief Chapter Twelve

In and Out and In and Out

I tried again.

When I was still a college boy, I tried "love" again, this time with a brooding, aspiring actor. His dry wit masked a pessimistic sincerity and, beneath that, a deeply sincere pessimism. I adored his darkness, convinced that my sunshine—my eternal, relentless, intrusive, desperately manufactured sunshine—would make him happier than he ever imagined wanting to be. While I bounced about seeking his approbation, he established that he was a wounded bird; in a rage, his father had once emptied a round of gunshot into an automobile engine that refused to start. My unhappy actor said all the things I needed to hear for my own drama, and he was a good actor, certainly better than I would ever be. He always got the details just right. He did so offstage, as well. He talked of the years we would share. With the latest issue of *The New Yorker* prominent on our tasteful coffee table, we would grow old together with intellectual panache and good-gay taste.

I bought an electric skillet and a copy of *Skillet Cooking for Two*. How was I to know that hubris could take the form of a countertop appliance? I never even considered that this relationship might not endure. Loving once, loving twice, sold forever. He would, in resonating tones, time without end, read aloud to me from the *New Yorker*, and I would endlessly ply him with perfectly fried chicken and modestly tossed salads of iceberg lettuce, served informally on that tasteful coffee table. Arm-in-arm, hand-in-hand, side-by-side, we would endure, over an eternity of fried foods, roughage, and timeless design.

The ending was a bewilderment belonging to us both. He walked away. Or did he run? In response, I wrote painful, pain-filled letters, embarrassing, obsessive, accusatory, and unforgivable. I was terrified then, and I think I still scare him.

I also suspect that I was not to him what he was to me.

Years later, I put our electric skillet out in the trash. Its Teflon-coated interior was scratched and gouged by years of solitary meals, its guaranteed non-stick surface no longer smooth. I gave up cooking, for myself and for anyone. My New York oven went unused for several decades.

In moments of self-indulgent morbidity, I used to imagine that I would someday be walking in a heavy snow storm, stop on a street corner, look up, and there he would be—the actor I still loved—sitting on a passing bus, oblivious to me, a light above him, illuminating his older but still attractive face. I would wave, but he would not see me. I would feel a new and terrible pain in my heart, sink down gently into the snow, and die, as he passed on in the traffic, unaware of my death. Or life.

Fade to black.

Later, I realized that my daydream was just a fantasy rip-off, slightly rearranged, of Omar Sharif's final moments in *Dr. Zhivago*.

In fact, the actor and I do email from time to time. I carefully close with "Fondly," which is one step past "Sincerely yours" and still safely distanced from "Love."

An old relationship looking for a "Complimentary Close."

As that second great love collapsed, I told myself that although he was a better actor, I was a better *entertainer*. I could cover up what I felt and sell that song to the back row.

I became Kentucky's answer to Betty Hutton. Kooky Kevin. Frantic.

I promised myself that I would fall in love again, but before my brain had reached its full adult functioning, I had hardwired it to associate love with obsession, unrealistic expectations, and prearranged rejection.

Two strikes had been enough to put me out.

Nonetheless, I kept swinging, inning after inning, with no merciful referee to throw me out of the ballpark, at least not for a long time.

I hope I am extending a coherent sport's metaphor. Still unsure. Still "not athletic."

There was a smooth dancing man, who again said whatever it took to make me melt into hope. Promises, promises. Talk, talk, talk, followed by a sudden and ominous silence. Pressed for some explanation, he told me that he met another man, said the same things to this man that he had said to me, but that with this other man, he had "meant them more."

Actors.

Maybe by then I was just acting, too.

For a while, I thought I was still looking for a relationship, a home for my heart. If love came close, however, I always ran away, fast, slamming doors behind me.

Someone gave me a bottle of champagne. I kept it in the back of my New York refrigerator for years, determined to open it only when I could share it with someone who said, "I love you," and to whom I could reply, "I love you, too." By the time I finally threw the bottle away, the champagne had turned to vinegar.

Something unpalatable.

Sour grapes.

Most of the theatre people I knew were kind. A few of them thought I had some talent as an actor and a singer. On stage, I played every possible variation of boyish virginity and had more "first kisses" than an all-female boarding school. I played "The Boy" in *The Fantasticks* and thought I knew what that boy was about. The open-hearted actress playing "The Girl" made me feel secure enough in my sexuality to play "straight" even if I wasn't. She was the first of a long line of similarly generous colleagues. I was grateful. On the few occasions that I had to play a love scene with an actress who only saw me as "some gay guy," my confidence crumbled, and I crawled through each performance in an agony of self-consciousness. I learned new lessons about self-respect and respect-withheld.

From time to time, offstage, I still caught myself struggling to be what I thought Kentucky thought I ought to be.

I finally tried *it* with madcap Rachel, losing my hetero-virginity to the sound of a spoken-word recording of *A Streetcar Named Desire* on my stereo turntable. The choice provided great resonance for an English major. We made love as terrified Blanche shouted, "Fire! Fire!"

Rachel was the character that Tennessee Williams forgot to create but did. She seemed to soak up all of the playwright's characters; she was prim Miss Alma, garrulous Amanda, dithering Blanche, desperate Maggie, needy Big Mama, glamorous Alexandra Del Lago, clueless Heavenly Finley, and a bit of Stanley Kowalski. She was an actor, artist, palm-reader, and belly-dancer.

Once, when I was home from New York visiting my parents in Kentucky, she showed up. Mother and Daddy were out. Rachel took a small suitcase upstairs and asked me to wait for her in my parents' living room. A few minutes later, a braceleted hand pushed a boom-box around a corner at the top of the stairs. A click and then an exotic rhythm. "Ca-ching, ca-ching, ca-ching. Ca-ching, ca-ching, ca-ching." A hand emerged, a leg, and then Rachel, descending the stairs, all swirling chiffon and undulations and finger cymbals. She may have been ululating. She was always the sort who might, entirely unprovoked, begin to ululate. She danced on. "Ca-ching, ca-ching, ca-ching." I heard a car in the driveway. Mother had returned home. Rachel's performance continued, with bumps, grinds, rotations, and tintinnabulation. Mother came into the room. I expected maternal sputtering, but she perched on the edge of her best wingback chair and watched Rachel bounce and shimmy. At last, the presentation ended.

A pause.

"Rachel, honey," asked Mother with placid curiosity, "do you know that you favor your left hip?"

"Drive around the corner, Kevin, and let me have another look."

Rachel later married, twice. On the back of her first wedding announcement, she wrote to me, "If this doesn't work out, we can still get married when we are forty."

Ca-ching!

In the meantime, I made out madly with Shirley at a New Year's Eve party, and I thought I might be in love with Joodi, a lady with lovely blue eyes, if odd spelling habits.

One afternoon after a few glasses of wine, Antonia and I kissed. I was immediately certain that we should get married. She knew that I was a gay man, but for a brief time the proposal seemed reasonable enough. I thought I had found a way out of confusion. I would not have been the first gay Kentuckian to trot selfishly down this path of wishful thinking. Sober, we didn't go in that direction.

Cheryl and I were in a few shows together. Backstage, we giggled and sang the "Nanny Song" from *Mary Poppins* together. Like sister and brother. Then, after a late-night bottle of white wine, we went "to bed together," as the expression used to go. Elegant and intelligent, Cheryl understood well how I was made. We shared a memorable night, but I did not know how to handle the aftermath. She sent a card with a line from Wordsworth. "The Child is father to the man."

Grow up, she suggested.

In an over-reaction, I told Mother that Cheryl and I might be getting married. Mother was cold. Unconvinced. Or I was unconvincing.

Grow up!

Each time, my equipment all hetero-worked, but I stopped "experimenting with women." The phrase, in itself, records a pursuit unworthy of a rational mind and moral soul. I learned to know myself better. Respect, learned and earned. The child fathered the man.

But I was not to be a father. No children. I wanted for a long time to pass on what my parents gave me. They were good parents, but, in the end, I did not want to pass on what the world had done to me.

I did, however, become a teacher.

CHAPTER THIRTEEN

COMING OUT TO BROTHER, SISTER, PARENTS, AND AN

ALL-BOYS' SCHOOL

I rarely thought about "coming out." When I wasn't home with my family, it hardly seemed necessary. As an adult, I was *out* to my closest friends without having to stage a confession. I was *out* when I worked in the theatre because it was assumed that all tenors, especially blond tenors, must be gay. The assumption, in my case, was correct. As time went by, I supposed that anyone who did not know that I was gay was just unable to face the obvious truth.

I supposed that meant most of my family.

I would have thought my brother knew. I certainly knew he was gay, although we did not discuss it until several years into college. In his room he curated a neat stack of *After Dark* magazines, arranged, typically for him, in order of publication. *After Dark* made a feeble pretense of being a magazine of the arts, but the photographs of shirtless actors and bare-assed dancers conveyed a message of little art and less artifice. As someone said, "Gay as a goose."

Goose?

To my big brother, I was still "Goose."

One evening, as his friends arrived to take him off to the smoky clubs of downtown Cincinnati, I asked to speak with my brother. He was well-dowsed in the peppery cologne that he taken to wearing when he "went out." I thought I was calm, but my words were awkward.

"I think we have the same problem," I said to him.

He was patient.

"I don't think of it as a *problem*," he replied. He then added that his friends had been asking if I "*was*." Some of them, he told me with a judicious display of dimples, thought I was "cute."

I asked for brotherly advice.

"It's mean out there, Goose," said my brother.

Our older sister stayed in Kentucky, and we assumed for too long that she might not understand or fully accept her gay brothers. Like ours, however, her life was an evolution and a revelation. She outgrew the "good old boy" sort, finding and marrying a gentle gentleman who appreciated her joyous spirit; they laughed together, like Ada and Albert. My brother and I had, of course, underestimated the generosity of our sister's nature.

When I was in my late-forties, my sister asked me several leading questions over lunch about a former friend, one who had long ago scorned me as "not athletic." Yes, I told her, sure, he was gay. Then, jerked into moral rectitude by the circumstances, I added that if I were to out others, I felt obliged to out myself. And so, I did. It took her a while to understand that my being gay did not give me magical powers in home decoration, fashion design, and gourmet cooking—R.I.P., electric skillet—, but telling her the truth was a relief to us both, not that she was surprised. She asked about our brother. I suggested she ask him. She did not. He had moved away from Kentucky, too, and he volunteered nothing. They would find the right time.

As I wandered into late middle-age, it became clear that I would not have my parents for many more years. Several times, I tried telling them that I was gay, but Mother always sensed what was coming and deftly blocked the conversation. For a woman who could worry a subject to exhaustion, like a dog circling chickens, she was quite adept at changing topics when she wished. Kentucky ladies are expert in redirecting conversations.

There was, however, an awkward close call.

One evening, when I was visiting home, I joined my parents after dinner to watch the national news on television. They were seated behind me, out of my line of vision, in their matching wingback chairs. I reclined, full length, on a long white sofa. The cat jumped up and settled herself on my legs. I was half-asleep when I heard my mother's sudden exclamation.

"Jaa-ack, just look at that big queen stretched out on the couch!"

My eyes snapped open, but the rest of me, body and soul, froze. I did not dare turn around. This was not what I had hoped for, not what I had imagined, and definitely not the way it was supposed to go.

A blushing moment later, of course, I realized that Mother was talking about the languid cat in my lap.

Nevertheless, I did not turn around. I pretended to be deep in sleep. This was not the night that would I would "come out" to my parents.

Eventually, however, I managed to sit them both down for "the talk." Mother sought delay, of course, but I pushed ahead. They sat again in their matching wingback chairs. Again, I was on the long white sofa. This time, I turned to face them both. Daddy looked intently at me. Mother set her face sternly, lips thin, but her eyes darted about nervously. I smiled, sighed, and gave it my best shot.

Partially rehearsed, but mostly improvised.

Certainly, from the heart.

I thought of that conversation in the restaurant when I was hung-over and emotionally smudged. Then, I was a victim. This time, I was in control, a bit defiant, nearly giddy, definitely unashamed.

I began by telling them that I loved them and that I was certain of their love. I told them that we needed to discuss something they both knew and that could not possibly be a real surprise or shock to either of them. I told them that if we did not have this talk, the silence would make me sad when they were gone.

A deep breath.

"I am your gay son," I said.

I did not add that I was one of two. I know something about discretion.

In a dramatic pantomime behind his back, Mother waved her hands at me and indicated that I might be giving my father a heart attack. He was, in fact, the calmest person in the room.

I told them that I was all too aware of the misinformation that still flew about Kentucky. I told them that my sexuality was as much a natural part of me as the color of my eyes. It was not a *choice*. It was not a *lifestyle*. It was *not* the result of aberrant parenting. And it was also not an *abomination* before any Lord in Heaven I cared to acknowledge. I told them that my being gay did not mean I was a pedophile, that pedophilia disgusted me as much as it did them. I explained that I did not hate women, that, in fact, I liked women, but that I also did not want to be a woman. I saw an unspoken worry in their faces. No, I quickly added, I was not HIV positive.

I thought of all the gay men who had endured *that* conversation with their parents.

Mother wanted to know if I intended to "put a sign in the front yard."

Well, no.

She asked if my sister knew.

Of course.

Had I told my niece?

No, but she's never been stupid, I said.

Did my niece's children know?

No, but when they learn to walk and talk with confidence, they would quickly figure it out and make no big deal about it.

I pointed out that the world outside Kentucky had changed and that Kentucky would catch up. Or so I hoped.

Mother never asked if my brother *knew*. I know that she knew that would have been an awkward question. She had to "take a break," she said, voice choking. She left the room. Not without respect and love, I thought, "Drama Queen!" Still, I knew she was doing the best she could manage.

I sat with Daddy Jack. After a moment, he asked if he might ask a personal question.

"Sure," I said.

"Kevin," he asked, "do you have anyone in your life?"

"No," I answered, "but that is the best question you could have asked, Daddy."

My father, good as any and far better than most.

I thought it had all gone better than I might have expected. And at last it was done.

That evening, I called my brother to tell him the news.

"You did *what*?" he said, with an edge I recognized from a lifetime of fearing a big brother's displeasure.

I waited, silent. My brother likes it when I say nothing.

"Well, I can guarantee one thing," he continued at last, "the subject will *never ever* be mentioned again."

He was more or less right.

And I still serve cashews in a silver dish.

In her later years, Mother's next-door neighbor was a gay landscaper from the Kentucky mountains. Across the road, lived two retired lesbians, retired, that is, from their careers. They were still lesbians.

"Mrs. Dearinger is surrounded by homosexuals," said one local wit.

The reply from a second wit: "She always has been."

When I was almost forty, I began my teaching career at a co-ed Catholic boarding school in Connecticut. There were other gay teachers, and there were gay students, but, Lord knows, —and the Lord, He *knew*—nothing was ever said. The headmaster was a confirmed bachelor; his private bathroom was decorated with pictures of the boys' swim team.

I was at the boarding school for four years. Back in New York City, the real world, I was losing friends almost weekly to AIDS. It was the worst of times. When I could, I would slip back for a death-bed visit or a memorial service, but at school I kept my grief private, knowing that I might lose my job if I were honest about my life and those I loved. One of the teachers I most admired told me that he had overheard some students saying, "Mr. Dearinger is a queer." He had immediately intervened, he told me, and explained to them that I was "sensitive and artistic but straight." Terrified that I would lose his friendship, I said nothing to correct him.

Oh.

I directed plays and musicals at the school, which I proudly enjoyed, but when a student hate-scrawled "Homo! Fag!" under my name on several posters, I took down the posters without comment and neared despair. I worried less about who had graffitied the signs than I did about who had seen them before I removed them. I loved my job, but I started to plan my escape.

Later, I taught at a boy's day school in Manhattan. For years, I kept quiet. That school's headmaster, I was told, "doesn't really care, but he doesn't like it to be too obvious."

"It."

I suppose I tried to be what is called "discreet," but with my students, I never pretended to be heterosexual, and I hope I

174

consistently challenged the homophobia I encountered. I came out to several "out" students, even if only after they graduated. I always apologized for my earlier silence. They were always gracious enough to say that they understood my circumstances. I hope that they did. I was aware of my cowardice. I still am.

After fifteen years of teaching at the boy's school and one especially egregious reference to "fags" from a sophomore boy, I boiled over and spilled out. I did not ask permission. My Teflon-coating had worn away.

"Is there anyone, *anyone* at all, in this class," I growled, "who does *not* know that I am a gay man?" Two hands went up. "Well, I'm sorry," I continued, with a look that said I wasn't, "but how stupid can you be!"

I could not have done that in Kentucky.

Kevin Lane Dearinger

Chapter Fourteen

More or Less Final

Whatever has happened, I have survived. Whatever has crippled me, I have more than once been called "high-functioning."

I am still around.

Given my blinkered innocence, it never ceases to surprise me that the worst of the Plague Years left me standing.

Several years ago, my Catholic high school in Kentucky refused to admit a lesbian couple to the prom. The senior class walked out of the official dance and held a protest prom in the parking lot to support and include the two young women. I wrote an earnest letter to the school's administration, asking how they could still sanction such prejudice and hate in their terrazzo-tough halls. My letter was never acknowledged. Daddy had died, but I sent a copy to Mother. She replied in vague terms, but I think she had begun to accept the possibility that my life has possessed some measure of dignity begat of eventual honesty. I'll say it again: Mother was never stupid.

For the last ten years of my teaching career in Manhattan, my school welcomed gay couples to its senior prom; did it help that I was the prom coordinator? The school's heterosexual athletic director served as the first advisor to the school's Gay-Straight Alliance.

Under the surface, however, festered old prejudices.

When I finally "came out" at school, the headmaster took me to lunch at one of his East Side clubs ("Men Only"). Clutching at the jargon of enlightened diversity, he thanked me for "sharing" my life with my students, but he could not look me in the eye and left me to finish my meal on my own. He also ordered me not to wear woolen scarves. I remembered the shame of short pants at a scorching sixth-grade picnic in Kentucky. "Not appropriate," said the headmaster, with a judgmental frown and frosty shake of the head.

Oh, the closeted paranoia of Park Avenue vacuity!

When I was hobbled by back pain and could only stand and sit with the help of a cane, I never missed a day at the school, but this same tinpot despot called me into his office to tell me that I was not to been seen using a cane in *his* school. The cane "sent the wrong message in a place of *vitality*." He meant, of course, "*virility*." I knew this drill well enough; it beat upon the bruise of old Kentucky guilt. With plenty of medical evidence to back up my need for the cane, I considered a lawsuit, but then I remembered a long-ago lesson. The bulldozers always have more money. By necessity, I continued to get myself to school each morning with a cane, but I pulled it up into my coat sleeve whenever I saw the bully who controlled my paycheck. I promised myself that I would outlast him at the school, and I did. *Quite* happily.

Still, the world spins mostly forward.

In 2013, I took the train to Boston and witnessed my brother's wedding. With a minimum of ceremony and fuss, he married his "long-term companion" at Boston's City Hall. "No big deal," said my brother, and yet our mother was not told. Our remarkable sister could not be there, but she arranged to treat us to lunch. My brother had "told" her at last. "How," he asked me, "did we come by such a wonderful sister?"

Great, great luck.

Each Sunday, I search out the gay wedding

announcements in the *New York Times*. The paper's editors indicate the individuals in the couple photographs as "left" and "right," their identities no longer obvious by appearance of gender. Sometimes I know the faces in the wedding photos. Actors. Musical Theatre actors. More and more often, however, the couples are doctors, lawyers, educators, gay men and women with jobs that in the past were not "gay-obvious," or, as in the case of teachers, were unthinkable for openly LGBTQ persons.

I often read these happy proclamations with tears in my eyes.

I used to cry, often, hard, and alone.

When I was bullied in school and dared not tell my parents, I would come home and sit in my room in my great-grandfather's rocking chair and weep away my frustration. Or I would curl up with our border collie, the softball-fielder, and cry into her soft fur. Good old dog! By the time I was in college, I rarely cried with any sort of unhappiness. I was more inclined to shake with dry sorrow or flinty rage. Or just sing louder and smile more broadly, selling *something* to the back row.

Now, if I cry, I usually cry for what is beautiful or perfect: the unexpected detail in a painting, the grace of great acting, the first measures of any string quartet, the fearless leap of an inspired dancer, light at noon through the leaves of an ash tree, a sudden kindness. Moments of perfection cue my tears. When Peter Pan flies, I get weepy and never see the wires. Walt Whitman's outreach to connect with the world, "filament, filament, filament," makes me cry. Paulina's invitation to Hermione in Shakespeare's *Winter's Tale* to end her marble exile, "t'is time, t'is time…be stone no more," makes me weep.

Things that are just right, just natural, choke my voice, drown my soul.

"Be stone no more."

I am still Charlie the Tuna, possessing a degree of taste yet never tasty. I have no realistic hopes of marriage. I keep my daydreams in the realm of the possible and change the topic when it crops up.

(A self-indulgent diversion.)
Our rooms are furnished as our souls
With bric-a-brac and dusty goals
And goods not good and books unread
And thoughts too quick we left for dead.
The beds and blankets promise rest
But prattled patience fouls the nest
And sleeplessness will wake and walk
The floor all night with unshared talk.
While universal pronouns stoop
Returning now in endless loop
And slowly drop pretense of we
Revealing solitary me.
The china sulks on shelves unused
And silver dulls as hearts abused
And all these *things*, come push to shove,
Are grim displacements and not love.

When I bought a cherry sleigh-bed, single mattress, a close friend commented, "That's a beautiful bed, Kevin. You'll sleep in that bed for the rest of your life. You'll die in that bed."

A single bed.

Daddy asked if I had someone. I don't. If questioned, my sister tells her friends, "Kevin just hasn't met the right one yet," but I stopped looking long ago. The "right one" has been banished by fears, nostalgia, and fantastical expectations.

We can never be again what we never were before.

Somewhere the image of Kevin with a partner, Goose with a Gander, disappeared from my head, and without an imagined lover, the real thing has found no open passage into my life, my heart, or my narrow bed. So be it.

Perhaps.

Ask me again when I am seventy.

But that others have someone that they can marry for love and with love, and that they *prove* with day-to-day devotion that it *is* love, this is what makes me cry.

My grandparents, my parents, and my sister married for love.

So did my brother.

Gay marriages have just begun to be acknowledged on the wedding pages in the Lexington paper, and even *The Woodford Sun* in Versailles has managed to acknowledge same-sex commitments, at least in obituaries. "Survived by a partner." Love in death. Love after death. Liebestod.

Mother and Daddy Jack are both gone, at least physically, but their dreams echo in my own. Our old home, their home, was sold to a back-to-the-farm gay couple. I am told that they keep horses, chickens, and pigs. They raise bulldogs. Mother and Daddy's old mortgage was long ago paid off, but now there is a new mortgage to be paid with new hopes. Mrs. Dearinger is still "surrounded by homosexuals." I hope she doesn't mind.

I retired from my first careers and from New York and returned to live full time in Kentucky. I own a quirky old home in Lexington. I love the town, with its complicated history and its complicated people. I am, however, still uneasy there. I still live a life that feels split, mis-fitted, halved by transience and the still-lingering sense of being "the other," the outsider. My penchant for nostalgia can conjure up some frightening ghosts.

Most of the gay men I know have a steady inner gauge, a sense of safety or danger. For most of our lives, when we have entered a new space, we have needed to determine if it might be a good place to be natural or a place that required pretense. In Lexington, I avoid dark streets and duck my head when marauding college boys drive by, throwing beer cans and invective out the windows of their trucks or BMWs. I still worry if I carry an umbrella or wear a woolen scarf on a wintery day.

Story One: In my mid-sixties, dressed in conservative clothing, minding my own business on Lexington's Main Street, thinking only of the lovely late-day sky, I am verbally assaulted, out of the blue in the Bluegrass: "Hey, fag. You're gonna die, fag. I hope you die, fag." Suddenly, I am thirteen years old again, a freak in Kentucky, a freak who just wanted to grow up to be a saint. I do not understand.

Story Two: I am in my mid-sixties, shopping in the Versailles Kroger Store. A local woman spots the reusable canvas bag I have brought from my car to avoid the waste of plastic. "Ooooooo," she sneers in a mock marvel, "and how long have you been carrying a purse, *Kevin?" I am shocked by the depth, breadth, and height of my angry response. So is she.*

But there has been progress in Kentucky.

Fayette County is a blue oasis in a desert of red-vulture voters; a lesbian in Manhattan once yipped in recognition when I mentioned Lexington. "Oh," she said with admiration, "the flannel-lesbian capital of the world!"

Lexington has a very active LGBTQ community. There are historical markers to honor its gay history, its downtown bars, and its Fairness Ordinance. The town has a Pride celebration each summer, out in the open, in front of the new courthouse. Versailles, too, has a Pride festival, nestled in a family park. Their advertising is "discreet." My birth-town, however, has also adopted a Fairness Ordinance, riddled with compromise, but well-intended and a step out of the darkness.

"Better than some."

There are still hecklers and haters. The "God Hates Fags" bigots and pathetic neo-Nazi buffoons show up at the edges of Lexington Pride gatherings; the younger LGBTQ folk glance at them without concern and carry on their celebration. I rage; I am an older gay man. A local fundamentalist church once hired an airplane to circle a Pride event with a banner promising Biblical damnation to the celebrants below. I told my companions at the time that the plane reminded me of the flying monkeys in *The Wizard of Oz* and the wicked witch on her broomstick, trailing plumes of green smoke. "Surrender Dorothy." The younger gay men did not recognize the reference. Or they pretended not to know.

"Who's Dorothy?"

Some of them don't seem to know much about what it used to be like to grow up gay in Kentucky, but I rejoice that their ignorance is a measure of their greater comfort in the world.

I know that there are others, in Kentucky, across America, and around the world, who still suffer far worse persecution than I ever did. My feeble razor blade did no more than nibble at my wrist. Something else triumphed within me.

Or I was just luckier than I thought I was.

Lexington now has openly gay judges, gay doctors, and even gay teachers in public schools, although the latter still move on soft-mittened feet. We had a popular and highly successful gay mayor. He can be spotted in local restaurants, dining with his partner. I have to wonder what my life might have been had I had such role models when I was trying to define my identity.

Meanwhile, my old Catholic high school still won't hire openly gay teachers. There are LGBTQ student-support groups (long time a-coming), but they have to meet quietly, although not as secretly as they did a year ago. Gay Catholics gather in Lexington, but they move with nervous prudence. The local "Bears," "Leather Daddies," the "Imperial Court" of supremely talented drag artists, and even the Pride celebration, all revel in openness, but still seem to seek some disguise, some label, a mask of make-up, muscle, facial hair, or moisturizer.

I admire choices but resist molds.

I am not a Jell-O salad.

Or is it that I am still ashamed to be an outsider?

So many gay people are still hiding, allowing their authentic selves to emerge only on weekends. There is still a penalty for being "obvious." There is still judgment, often self-inflicted. One mountain boy, relocated to Lexington, has a removable "rainbow" bumper-sticker on his pickup truck: there for weekends, off for workdays at the plant and visits home in the hills. Not quite the rainbow that made the hearts of Wordsworth and Harvey Milk leap up.

But I listened with pride, real pride, to a Pride Day speech, delivered by an "out" senior from my old homophobic high school. He was just a boy, a natural, happy, smiling, glad-to-be-himself boy, and, yes, I cried. I hope I will always cry in the presence of such glory.

Kentucky continues to be an odd place, or at least a place that makes me feel *odd*. Our state song remains a beautiful ballad, but its lyrics have long been problematic. "The sun shines bright on my old Kentucky home," it began when I was younger, "'tis summer, the *darkies* are gay." For years we all avoided eye contact as we mumble-sang the offensive word. Eventually, the racist term was officially replaced with "people." Now, when Kentuckians stand and sing their lovely anthem, their eyes glaze over, and they still mouth the phrase gingerly, "'tis summer, the people are gay." At a recent event in Lexington, the too-loud gentleman leading the singing of the state song apologized for the word, explaining, "It doesn't mean *that!*

"*Heh-heh-heh!*"

That same old dirty laugh.

Well, a good many Kentuckians are, in fact, gay, but so many of the gay men I know now in Kentucky talk too much (for me) about "tops" and "bottoms." Categories, not individuals. They speculate on the sexual identities of celebrities, repeating rumors of those among the famous who have been "seen in a gay bar," all in tones of derision. They won't speak of HIV and don't want to hear about HIV. By night, they flock to local drag shows but won't acknowledge transgender people in the light of day. "Not cool." They brag about their "straight-acting" boyfriends, while calling each other "girl" or "bitch." They casually describe the heartless hook-ups they arrange online. They advertise their availability, twittering what they want and how they want it.

Now. Now. Now.

Pleasure ground out on Grindr.

"No fats, no femmes, and *no old men.*"

They talk about sports and "go to all the games." They watch Saturday night basketball on ESPN and then go to The Bar and drink enough to dance with abandon and maybe get lucky. They still drink to be "free." The next day, in rumpled clothes, they wander home or directly to brunch.

Bars bore me. Tales of sexual conquest bore me. Sport's talk has always bored me. I prefer plays to play-offs. I was never athletic in the Commonwealth of Kentucky.

And I don't care.

God help me, I never really did.

I know that I was a "good boy," but I wasn't very good at being a *boy* in Kentucky. Now I find that I am not all that good at being a gay *man* in Kentucky. I have seen and heard too much. I work diligently just to try to be a good *person.* Period. Full stop. That's enough of a challenge.

I will conclude with a trumpet's blast, a long-simmering jeremiad:

In my human heart and despite the chains on my Catholic soul, I believe my sexuality is natural.

My sexuality is honorable.

My life is my own.

Love is not sex.

Sex is not love.

They can co-exist, and each, at times, is necessary for human happiness.

My often-tender brother has suggested to me that for all of my musings about "bad" sex in Kentucky, there must have been some good sex along the way, or we would not be so decidedly here. As usual, he's right. There has been plenty of sex that was fulfilling and satisfying to all involved, and sex that passionately expressed shared respect, shared lives, and shared love. Good sex in Kentucky.

I am the progeny of furrowed fields and furrowed brows, cold farmhouse kitchens and dark whorehouse halls, Hollywood kisses once-removed and misguided doctors, Freedom-riders and the lynch mob.

I am the descendent of Baptist denial and Catholic presumption, gospels and epistles, Leviticus, Acts, and Revelations.

I am the result of derision and indecision, settlements and discontent, self-satisfaction and relentless need.

I am the product of bullies and cowardice, teachers and heroes, fiction and non-fiction, bourbon and branch water, prose and poetry, parental warmth, memory, and forgetfulness.

I am the son of Stonewall and Streisand, Dr. Spock nurtured, and Mr. Spock inspired. *"Live long and prosper."*

I am witness to a great quilted lawn, embroidered with the names of the dead, and a mourner for generations gone, family and friends, and gutted address books.

I am part and product of something indefinable but which some have called love.

I haven't been a virgin for a very long time, but something unsullied still streaks my heart. My dreams are rarely erotic now, but I often dream of the pure warmth of a human embrace.

I am the child of Kentucky land and Kentucky legend.

I am the natural outcome of "mixed parties."

"T'is time, t'is time… be stone no more."

Bad Sex in Kentucky

More from
RABBIT HOUSE PRESS

Cinderella Sweeping Up
Erin Chandler

Junebug Versus Hurricane
Erin Chandler

Biloxi Back Bay: Selected Poems of Rob Greene
Rob Greene

Transcendental Voyages: From Kentucky to Kathmandu
Nancy Royden

Made in the USA
Middletown, DE
13 November 2019